THE GLORY SIGNS

(NEW WRITING SCOTLAND 16)

Edited by

KATHLEEN JAMIE
and
DONNY O'ROURKE

with Rody Gorman (Gaelic Adviser)

Association for Scottish Literary Studies

Association for Scottish Literary Studies
c/o Department of Scottish History, 9 University Gardens
University of Glasgow, Glasgow G12 8QH

First published 1998

British Library Cataloguing in Publication Data

A CIP record for this book is available
from the British Library

ISBN 0–948877–37–5

THE SCOTTISH ARTS COUNCIL

Typeset by Roger Booth Associates, Hassocks, West Sussex

Printed by Bell & Bain, Glasgow

CONTENTS

INTRODUCTION

Again we take pleasure in presenting *New Writing Scotland*, the annual finger-on-the-pulse of the literary nation. If aliens from the planet Zog, or indeed our closer neighbours, wanted to know who we were – the Scots, the people of this re-emergent wee nation, they could dae waur than look in any recent volume of NWS. Rural and urban, white and Asian, English and Scots and Gaelic speaking, poets and story-tellers, dour and quirky, our only consistency is variety.

For the editors, Spring is a clamourous time. The postie humphs several hefty boxes up the stair, and we start reading. Soon our heids are dinging. Four hundred voices, or thereby, are asking for a hearing, in all the languages of the land.

Each editor serves three years, long enough to sense fashions passing and developments beginning; short enough to ensure that one person's ideas don't dominate. It is not possible, however, for an editor of this volume to arrive with an agenda in mind. We can only go with the flow, trying to be alert to the shifts in culture. We're chuffed when we publish a new writer for the first time, equally chuffed when a writer of considerable reputation submits something special. Whoever the author, whatever the technical skill, we choose those pieces of work which have life about them. Themes emerge through some mysterious means of their own. One year will be strong for landscape poetry, say. The next will yield an unexpected crop of gay writing. This volume, as chance would have it, is graced by several strong pieces about the experience of bereavement.

Welcome to *New Writing Scotland 16*. This year, when change is afoot in our country; well we might ask: who are we, what are we? This book may not provide the answer, but its many and various voices provide a sign. We believe it's a healthy sign for the future, who knows, perhaps even a Glory Sign.

Finally with *New Writing Scotland 16*, Managing Editor, Catherine Mc Inerney, signs off after five years. Her contribution to the series and to ASLS has been enormous. It has been a pleasure to work with her and we wish her all the best in her new job as Scotland's first Literature Development Officer. She will be missed.

Kathleen Jamie
Donny O'Rourke

Ken Angus

MIDWEEK BREAK: HELENSBURGH, MAY 1945

The morning sun was extra bright the day
that peace broke out. We waited for our boat
on Tarbert pier, sensing the interplay
of gulls and herring, nets and creosote.

Feeling ridiculous in shorts and blazers,
we sat in a torpedo-boat, drank tea
sweeter than syrup, brewed by cheerful sailors,
then off to Tighnabruich, Hunter's Key

and Craigendoran. Mingling on Clyde Street,
crowds of people laughed and talked; the bliss
was almost palpable. I rushed to greet
my parents: felt Dad's hand-clasp, Mother's kiss.

Wonders were scooped from carefully-hoarded tins:
our butter rations squandered at a stroke
for making sandwiches; ice clinked in gins
-and-tonics; the air was blue with cigar-smoke.

In panorama, far across the bay,
dear Greenock sparkled like the Milky Way.

Gavin Bowd

MUNGO

Three centuries past
We do not know you.

Silence plants its bark
Around our exchanges.

Our cloth, your gold.
Our guns, your ivory.
Our goods, your slaves.

We catch glimpses of
Your scarlet gums
And plunging throat.
Your temples thrum.

Miles of lip
Stroked by the Atlantic.
Tightly sealed.

After so much time
We do not know you.

*

We are experts.
We will be discrete.

We will offer our minds
Without interest.

*

These muscles run on
Predestined blood.

Confident that the reins
Of events are in
Our Father's hands.

*

Mungo learns Mandingo
Then takes a slave interpreter:

You will carry my words
To the end of the Niger.

Then you will be free.

*

We dress as we would
Back home.
We do not pretend.

We know that this region
Can eat our skins.

*

Perhaps quitted forever
Christian comforts.

*

The King of Fatteconda
Finds it impossible

That so many dangers could be faced
Merely to look.

*

I see no differences
Between the races.

They sweat as much
As me in my waistcoat.

We both hate the bees.

*

I was captured by the Moors
Of Ludamor.

They confined me to a tent
Where a pig was tethered.

A cloud of flies
Judged the unclean.

*

The interpreter
Has dumped me.

He has regained his family
Behind the trees.

*

An irritation spreads
Across my back.
My scalp is itching.

Blisters reveal
The strangest pus.

This skin has eaten
A continent's dirt
And become rough.

*

Escape meant the desert's
Mortification.

Until the clouds poured grace
That I wrung and sucked
From my clothes.

Before me swelled the Niger
Running to the East.

*

Sego.

Civilisation and magnificence
I little expected to find
In the bosom of Africa.

Black female nudity
Stares at me,
Eyes large as nipples

'Let us pity the white man.
No mother has he.'

*

Vast wilderness.
Naked and alone.

Savage animals and men.

Deliverance
From a benevolent Negro.

*

I astonish even
The educated ones.

I should have worn
Native dress,
Learned Arabic.
What would I trade?

Travel for its own sake
Is incomprehensible.

*

The slaves of the caravan
Are eager for answers:

'Have you really got
Such ground as this
To set your feet upon?

And when we have finally
Crossed the salt water,
Will they eat us?'

*

Back home they appreciate
My accounts of the interior.

They enjoy the prose style,
Reflective of my character.

Precise like a scientist.
Restrained like a sober Scot.

Yet they dislike my manner
And do not offer invitations.

*

At the Africa Society's
General Meeting,
1799,
Sir Joseph Banks declares:

'We have already by Mr Park's means opened
a Gate into the interior of Africa into which it
is easy for every nation to enter and extend its
Commerce and Discovery from the West to the
Eastern side of that immense continent.'

Send soldiers and field guns.
Build forts along the Niger.

Guerre à Napoléon
Et aux Français!

*

In Peebles, I apply
My surgeon's knife
To client skins.

Long rich veins
Of cysts and gouts.
Rain-bleached flab.

And one evening I broke
The promised seal
Of my childhood sweetheart.

*

When the cutting is done,
I pore over Golbey's
Fragments d'un voyage en Afrique.

Our men have captured
Goree from the French.

The crevice of the Gambia
Has burst its stitches.

*

Banks is behind us:

'Whoever colonizes in that part of Africa with
spirit will clearly be able to sell Colonial
Products of all kinds in the European market
at a cheaper price than any part of the West
Indies can afford it.'

*

This time we will follow
The Niger to its end.

We will rely on Europeans.
There will be no interpreters.

*

The knots of branches
Mock our hacking.

Our men are the dregs.
They shit themselves dry
And take epileptic fits.

The bees send them running
Into the trees
Wrapped in the Union Jack.

*

King Mansong
Had some consoling words:

'If you speak of a good gun, who made it?
The White people.'

*

We intended to build
A ship for the coast
But were ambushed.

We each take a European
And jump into the river.

*

Slave Fatoma says:

'They are all dead, they are lost forever.'

*

Thomas sets out
To find his father
Then dies of fever.

*

In the future we will be
More systematic.

Tom Bryan

POSTCARDS FROM ASSYNT

i) Autumn Loch

The sky is broken slate. Two men row a boat on the loch. Their yellow oilskins glisten with fish slime. They lift the long bag of a fyke net from the water. It is full of fish.
Life: two men deep in trout.
Death: the local lochside graveyard.
The Gaelic letters on the gravestones are covered by lichen. The numbers are illegible. The men row to the shore where the gravestones reflect the moon. The fish bump the bottom of a plastic bucket, seeking deeper water. The men, boat and loch are the same colour as the sky (which is now the same colour as the graveyard).

ii) Assynt Birch Forest

The birches resemble a natural picket fence along the crumbling dyke. The sun streams through the birch leaves and branches, speckling the ground with wind-riven shadows, as the tree leaves rustle. Mushrooms fleck the ground: chanterelles like orange peels, boletus like polished shoes, the red puke of fly agaric. The moss is knee-deep, blotched with dead birch leaves. A woman picks mushrooms in a shaft of sun; her tangled hair is a dark sea-wrack. Two thin birches swallow her shadow.

iii) Roadside

A buzzard fluffs on a deer fence strainer. Puffs out, preens, swivels. The bird is foreground, full against the background loch. The larches are bare, highlighting the white fingers of birch. The buzzard dives backwards into an updraft, seeking food in sullen ditches. My camera shutter flushes two black-birds from the dead bracken.

Moira Burgess

RACHEL

She's standing by the window looking out at the scene he knows so well: the heavy summer-leafy trees within the railings, the private gardens, to which he doesn't have a key. Stepping up the hill go the honey-coloured buildings of the square, each tall house a hive of secret thoughts, of acts you'd never dream of behind the high windows rose-stained by sunset light. He doesn't know what goes on in any of these houses, but he thinks that Rachel does.

Might all that be important? He pushes the thought away. At this moment, in this quiet room, only Rachel is important. Rachel, and what she's going to say.

Her slim hand holds back the velvet curtains and he sees the painted nails. She's lovely, long hair carelessly cut, dark-red slip dress that shows her shoulders and legs. She's a bit like Rachel in *Friends*, he's always realised, but where's the harm in that? She's been standing there for a long time.

'Come on,' he says. 'This is no use.'

She turns to look at him and he thinks she might speak, but no. She presses her lips together and turns to the window again. She's waiting for a phone-call: what it will say she doesn't know, and neither does he. How she'll react to it, equally, he doesn't know. 'I don't know much about you, do I?' he says. 'Maybe that's been the trouble all along.'

Still she doesn't speak; he recognises with a dragging sadness how seldom she speaks to him. He ought to get more help from her. He never hears her true voice. How much of this is his fault? Is it something he's done or something he's failed to do? 'Who are you, really, Rachel?' he says.

Now he's addressing her directly and he can't seem to stop. 'What's the matter with you? This is stupid! It's gone on far too long!' He's shouting, and of course it's done no good. He feels like a fool. They'll be able to hear him through the wall if they're in, and already they think he's strange. 'Why won't you do as you're told?' he screams.

She doesn't respond to that. Well, what woman would? There's a brief blink of understanding in his mind, but he can't catch it, it's gone. 'This is hopeless,' he says.

The phone rings and he snatches it up. 'We're in the pub,'

calls Becky, shouting over a chatter of voices, laughter, song.
'Me and Mick and Claire and everybody. We're going up to
Claire's after. Want to come?'

'No. Not just now.'

'Sure? Sounds as if you need a break,' Becky is bossily
diagnosing, but he bangs the receiver down. I'm nearly there
with Rachel, he wants to say. But you can't say that, or only to
a very few people, of whom Becky isn't one. Mick might
understand; there have been hints that Mick has been this way
before. Some night, perhaps over a pint, they'll find the words,
share the experience. Normally he doesn't talk about it. You
don't. It's so very nearly a sexual thing.

Across the room, though, Rachel moves. She picks up the
phone and makes a call. Who's she calling? His heart beats
hard in his throat. He hadn't expected this.

He sees her hands, stronger than he'd thought, and her
nails are unpainted after all. She's older than he thought, too,
he realises in a moment of wonder. Something about her eyes
speaks of what she's done and seen. Perhaps she's ringing
someone just across the square. Behind the sunset windows
someone is moving to pick up his phone.

'See you in the pub,' she says. Unheard and still unknown,
far away but near, the man, if it's a man, evidently demurs.
Rachel is looking out of the window as if she can see him.
Perhaps, across the square, he's looking at her.

'In ten minutes,' Rachel says.

It's right, what she does, what she says. Her move, her
initiative; that's the breakthrough. And the gardens, they do
have a part to play. Something has happened in the gardens.
Soon he'll know what it was, though it needn't be spelled out
for a while.

He keys it all in; later he'll attend to her fingernails. Black
varnish perhaps? She moves to the door, smiling for a reason he
doesn't yet understand, and he waits happily, sitting relaxed in
front of the computer, for Rachel to take him where she wants
to go.

John Clifford

THE BERDACHE SPEAKS

Just imagine:
there I was, sitting at my loom,
weaving.
And this man came in. Distracted me. He was wearing
trousers.
(These barbarians have no shame)
Watching me. Muttering under his breath.
Writing in a book.
**'An Account of the Manners and Customs of the Native
North Americans, or Redskins.**
It must be confessed that in these parts effeminacy and
lewdness are carried to the greatest excess. Men are seen to
wear the dress of women without a blush. And seen to so
debase themselves as to perform those occupations peculiar to
that sex. From this follows a corruption of morals past all
expression.'

He did seem a bit upset.
But I couldn't understand a word he was saying.

'These creatures are termed berdache.
From the French **bardache.** And the Italian **barbascio.**
And the Spanish **bardajo.**
Meaning: catamite.
The most degraded form of human life.'

I was thirteen when my vision came.
My clan were hunters, yet
I could not dispatch the deer felled by the arrow
or the fish writhing on the river bank.
My heart would twist with pity and my strength would fail
me.
And I knew that on the war path I could never kill a man.
I longed to perform the tasks that women do:
sit at the loom, cast pots and cultivate the earth.
This troubled me.
I implored the spirits for guidance.

'They sit among the women and spin. They wear women's
dress and ornaments.
Yet they are clearly men. And they sit and they spin and they
have no shame. To report this strains credulity yet I must.
For I have seen it. I have seen it with my eyes. And they have
the effrontery to claim this all comes from I know not what
principle of religion.
From this it can readily be seen this whole people are
irredeemably debased.'

The moon came to me
she came dressed in white
she held a bow and arrow in her right hand
in her left a woman's burden strap
one is the path of men
and the other is the woman's
I understood this, I saw this clearly,
and a voice said: Choose.
My arm reached for the bow, as I'd been taught
but I reached for the burden strap with my heart.
When I looked down to see what I was holding in my hand
I saw it was the burden strap.

I had chosen women's ways.
The spirits had approved my choice
and my heart was glad within me.
I went to the elders. I renounced men's clothes.
I wore women's dress and I performed the women's tasks
and my days of hiding were over.

'As Christians these are practices we can only abhor.
We can only be grateful in our hearts that the truth has been
vouchsafed us. And we can only pray for the strength to
disseminate it.'

I weave baskets. I paint pictures in the sand.
I am honoured among my people.
I sleep with the warriors when they need solace
I sleep with the women when they need strength.
The women give me courage: the men give me tenderness.
Both give me pleasure and both give me joy.

'There is profound gender malfunction here'
– and now the man had a white coat on –
'a chronic confusion of gender roles.
We could offer surgery. Remove the genitals that cause
you so much pain.
Give you classes in make up and deportment
Teach you to do your hair in a more becoming style.
So you look a little less conspicuous.
Frankly, just now, you don't look like a woman at all'

Why should I look like a woman? I am not a woman.

'Then learn to be a man'

I am not a man.
I am becoming! I am transformation! I am change!

'No this is all profoundly incorrect.
There is a universal human mind: and mind has to categorise.
There are categories of gender. You must belong to one of them.
You have to choose.'

I have chosen. I am who I am.

But he would not hear me. He just babbled on.
About binary opposition and correct gender roles.

We were in the badlands then
A day's journey from the waterhole.
I offered to guide him, but he refused.
I had to leave him, in the barren sands,
under the open pitiless sky.

And there I left him.
Howling.

Ken Cockburn

RECRUITMENT

Of course it won't be easy: if it was,
it wouldn't be exciting.

Technically we had him: the contract was watertight
and we could have bankrupted him overnight.
But we wanted him back in the ranks,
venting his belligerence on the competition.

We faxed him, upping the money and doubling the perks,
adding a share-option package better
than the one the CEO took all the flak for in the press –
his wife phoned on his behalf, declining.

In human terms, it means
breathing pure intellectual oxygen
working right at the frontiers of the possible
enjoying the satisfaction – and the rewards –
of knowing that you're making a difference.

He'd always liked to run things from home,
this hick island his grandfather had been smart enough
to dupe the peasantry out of.
He hadn't budged in near-on two years,
since the last big takeover battle.
Just him, the wife and the boy. He said
he'd had enough of that cut-throat world. He said
his shrink had told him if he got involved again
it'd take him maybe twenty years to get straight.

At the outset of your career but nonetheless
with relevant experience, you could join a project
that's attracted some of the most inspirational brains
in this or any other business –
figures of an almost legendary status.

So we paid a visit. Some journey:
two flights and a tortuous drive,
then he wouldn't send the helicopter.
It took a day to get the locals to agree
to ferry us across: another till we sailed,
high winds and the tides against us, so they said,
and inauspicious portents in the tea-leaves, for all I know.

The CEO was incandescent at being snubbed
at kicking his heels in the back of fucking beyond,
at not getting a strong enough signal
to instruct HQ to launch injunctions like Cruise missiles –
the Chairman calmed him down, saying
we were playing the long game,
a game we couldn't win without the dream-team.

Unflagging energy, total intellectual honesty
the ability to tell consensus from compromise
credibility with top client management
as much as with your own peers –
qualities like these will underwrite your success.

He played the fool. Offered coffee
and served rum; offered biscuits
and served saucerfuls of rabbit turds.
Excused himself, he had to mow the lawn:
drove his tractor the length of the beach,
the trailing blades ploughing up a sandstorm.

I asked the boy to take us down to him.
The first time, he drove so close we got facefuls of sand.
The next time I caught the boy off-balance,
nudged him, and he fell, I thought, among the blades.
But the brakes were on before he hit the sand
and the madman cursed us so sincerely
nobody doubted the mask was off.

In essence, what we're offering
is the opportunity to make a visible contribution
to a project that's of fundamental importance
to one of the world's great epics –
a project that will still be talked about years from now.

We got down to business on the helicopter.
He doesn't talk about the island,
but I've seen him address the odd letter there.
Nowadays he's back to his old self,
knocking heads together. Tomorrow
we go public.

Of course it won't be easy: if it was,
it wouldn't be exciting.

Stewart Conn

THE MOSQUITO SONATA

Everything round him was white. And tented. As if he lay within a huge bridal veil, its folds overhanging and spilling out so that they enveloped him. And there it was again. He tried moving his head, but it felt clamped. He could do nothing. To stop that high-pitched whine, its continuous insinuating note...

*

Messiaen incorporated birdsong into his music. For a piece of his own he'd made a recording of a blackbird, played it back at slow speed, and transcribed it for flute. One smart-arse young critic denounced it as a 'cheep frippery'. Subsequent chamber works, even if well received in the concert hall, tended to be dismissed by similar *soi-disant* arbiters of taste. He saw himself as splayed on the altar of fashion. Underlying all, what they really resented was his *tunefulness*. Be more austere, was their cry. Minimalism *à la mode*. Reductionism is all. The new Reich.

The paintings he could relate to were representational. As for those Turner shortlists, he couldn't stomach their sensationalised excrescences. Similarly he saw the whole function of musical composition as pleasure-giving and life-enhancing, through its use of *melody*. Surely it should define character, tap and convey *feeling*. Was it his fault those ageist young whippersnappers couldn't respond? Far less relish his drawing on folk-tune? Although he'd changed of late. Had to. Since his little scare. It had been a narrow shave, right enough. Physically and metaphorically. His doctor had deserved credit for detecting and responding so speedily to the initial symptoms. Making sure he was in the right place when the first aneurysm occurred.

He'd come here to recuperate. Which is why he was now relaxing in the shade, in a hammock, in a Tuscan garden. A chilled Bianchetto Frizzante on a walnut table by his side. Clear skies above. Evenings lolling in the pool. A far cry from the East Neuk! But the rebukes kept nagging him. They'd had an effect, in that his music had changed. His outlook, too. His priorities seemed different now. He'd tried to cut out the 'fripperies'. Until paring things down had itself become something of an obsession. His aim now, to achieve – and leave to posterity –

something that had its own perfection, its own sparseness, its own purity.

Again the sound. Unmistakably, a mosquito. He flailed out. Missed. Some wine spilled from his glass. Woops, he thought, be careful. He raised his hand again, then froze. That was it! The answer. The ultimate! A single sound, austere... related to a live thing. The attenuation his life had become... was reduced to... Yes, he would write a sonata in the form of a single sustained note... right at the top of the instrument's range. How practical would it be? No worries there. His companion would have no difficulty with E, two octaves above the stave. Finger held high on the string. Failing that, perhaps the oboe. That would need circular breathing, though: difficult to sustain, at the top of the register. Hadn't Honneger something like this in one of his less train-like pieces? But a sense of strain was the last thing he'd want. Better stick to the fiddle...

Birtwhistle made a name for himself, for hitting high notes. But they positively *shrieked*. No, he'd be up there with John Cage. The last-crotchet saloon, prior to silence! He envisaged the audience sitting in anticipation. The soloist would begin, and keep going... and going... The **mosquito sonata** he'd call it. Derived from the sound of the insect prior to striking. A distillation of his whole life. Its intricately interweaving threads, and relationships, severed one by one. Down to a single tenuous strand. Those whipper-snappers. Minimalist? He'd show 'em! He blinked. Was what he was hearing in his head, or in the atmosphere? Was it the mosquito, preparing to attack? He looked round. The sound swivelled with him. As if the insect had entered his cranium, and was swelling there. Bigger and louder... so that before he could prevent himself, he had let his glass slip and put up both hands to cover his ears. Except of course, if the sound was *inside*, this would prevent its release, not...

Only now did he feel the pain. Excruciating. As if his skull was on fire. From the window, his companion saw him tear at his hair and writhe so that the hammock tilted and buckled, toppling him to the ground. The whining was cut short by a sharp crack. How funny. And appropriate. With its options how to end the piece. The plucking – or severing – of a single string, as the creature bit? Even more fitting, a terminal percussion-crash as it received its death-smack. At this the skin tightened across his mouth in what was meant as a mirthless smile, but to the observer might appear more a grimace, a rictus setting rapidly into a mask.

His companion came frantically running from the house to find him spread-eagled on the grass: beside him the wine-glass, unscathed and still containing its dregs. In no time he had been carried to the coolness of his room. There to be laid on his bed, the billowing mosquito-net drawn carefully round him. Barely conscious he stretched out, grasped its white mesh. Not realising he was trying to let an intruder out, his companion leaned across and pressed down the folds so that no slightest gap remained. The persistent whine now unbearable, he felt his whole life contained in (or reduced to) its unwavering note. His hand feebly struck then fell; to reveal on his temple the squashed breakage of legs and wings, and a thin smear of blood. Simultaneously giant hands gripped, as the massive haemorrhage took its toll.

Robert Crawford

NELSON

My father was always good with money, but money was never
his first choice. He told me he would like to have been a Church
of Scotland minister, like his own father, but it saddened him at
school that he could not manage Greek. He went to a number
of schools, including one in Stirling which had its own observa-
tory with a telescope tower extending from the roof, but he
thought of himself as having been educated in Aberdeenshire. I
still have two novels by R.M. Ballantyne which my father won
as prizes in his final year at school there. One is *The Young Fur-
Traders* in the Herbert Strang's Empire Library Series. It is set in
the limitless adventure-land around Hudson's Bay. 'Snowflakes
and sunbeams, heat and cold, winter and summer, alternated
with their wonted regularity for fifteen years in the wild regions
of the Far North.' The label inside the front endpapers reads,

Session 1927–28
Alford Public School
2nd Prize
R Nelson Crawford
Adv. Div. I
for
Excellence in Latin
James Ritchie M.A.
Headmaster

The other prize is for Perfect Attendance.

After he died, I discovered that my father had quietened me
with a small white lie. He had been expected to go on to
Inverurie Academy in 1930 to study Classics, before training for
the ministry at Aberdeen University. Mr Ritchie had been giving
him lessons after school. Though Dad once told me that Greek
had been too difficult for him, the truth was that at this time my
grandmother became totally blind and the family faced financial
uncertainty. My grandfather, who had worked in a central-belt
mining parish during periods of strikes, had given away his
savings to his parishioners and was left with scant funds. In the
circumstances, my father decided to stay on at home. I realise
now why he was so pleased when I studied Greek.

My father left school at sixteen. It was the era of the Depression and work was hard to come by, yet his mid-teens were probably among the happiest times of his life. For two years he lived on in the big manse with his elder brother, sister, and parents, while he bred Shetland ponies and pastured them on the large glebe. In late summer he would go grouse-beating, mixing with gillies and gamekeepers' sons. He kept hens too, rearing them and selling their eggs. My favourite book of his is dated 'Manse of Alford, Aberdeen, 1930' and contains illustrations of Light Sussex Cocks and Dark Dorkings. It is called *The Poultry Keeper's Vade Mecum.*

Shortly after this period, my grandparents managed to find my father a profession. They encouraged him to join the Union Bank of Scotland, sure that even in lean times banking was a secure and respectable career. John, his elder brother, became a policeman, got his own motor bike, and by all accounts was a bit of a lad. My father, though, was quieter, with gentlemanly, almost feudal manners. His parents had to pay the Bank to employ him – a bit like purchasing an apprenticeship. Work was so scarce in 1932 that he was the only person taken on by the Bank in the whole Aberdeen district. Apart from war service, my father would work for the Bank over the next forty years.

To start with, he lodged in Aberdeen, occasionally cycling to Alford and back in the summer – a distance of twenty-eight miles each way. He shared digs with two other young men, Alan MacInnes and Jimmy Russell. Alan, who had a reputation for taking two cakes at once when the plate was passed round, later became City Chamberlain of Aberdeen. Jimmy Russell was a photographer for the *Press and Journal.* When not at work, my father would sometimes accompany him, holding his tripod or other equipment while Jimmy photographed scenes of crimes, fires and accidents. Through Jimmy he was introduced to a very different world from that of the large country manse.

Too young to vote, yet with a clear career structure ahead of him, my father enjoyed being the youngest member of his office's professional staff. One of the Union Bank posters of the time shows a boy with a satchel sitting at his desk, writing with a pen and ink, as his pipe-smoking father looks on. 'When he reaches 21,' the caption reads, 'what a start he'll have with a Union Bank Deposit Account.' Another poster, which my father remembered in his eighties, showed a black and white cat, and read, 'You haven't 9 lives, so enjoy this one; let the Union Bank help you. Call today and open a Deposit Account with 1/- or More.' As the office junior, Dad was often sent to outlying local offices to 'do relief' while staff were on holiday or otherwise absent. He remembered taking the money in a big cash-box from the Braemar Gathering. At Aberlour, while the manager, who lived in the Bank house, dug potatoes in his back garden, my father could sit in his padded chair with a loaded shotgun, blasting at rabbits from the manager's office window. If an important customer arrived, it was Dad's job to relay this news down the garden, so the manager could then retie his tie and slip his hip-flask into his back pocket.

My father liked the contact with local people that banking gave him. All his adult life he was able to converse with anyone he met. It was customary to have long chats over the counter in the bank when business was quiet. Particularly in country districts, the banker had an intimate working relationship with his customers whom he saw on a daily or at least a week-to-week basis. At the same time, my father studied dutifully for his professional exams since without passing these he could not be promoted. There was no longer time for Shetland ponies, hens, or books about them. Instead, in the evenings he had to read works such as *Principles of Mercantile Law* and *Cordingley's Guide to the Stock Exchange*. On the one hand, he was paid very little; the bank controlled much of his personal life; male employees were not allowed to marry until they earned a substantial salary, so that they and their households might uphold the Bank's standards of respectability. On the other hand, the Bank's insistence on those standards meant that it was willing to pay employees' rent bills to ensure that they lived in 'digs' of appropriate quality. This meant that for several years during the 1930s my father's rent (paid by the Bank) was considerably in excess of his annual salary. That was regarded by the Bank as quite reasonable and in keeping with business propriety. The Bank did not recognise trade unions. A strike called for 30 April 1937 fizzled out almost as soon as it started. Its leader was promptly dismissed.

While my father was working in Darvel, Ayrshire, at the end of the 1930s, the Bank made it clear that no one who volunteered for the armed forces would be guaranteed his job back after the War. However, employees who waited for their call-up papers would be treated differently, and would be reinstated when the conflict ended. Dad marked time until he was called up, but he had already made enquiries about the Scots Guards at a recruitment office in Darvel. He joined that regiment and was soon given commando training. Though he had spent all his summer holidays in the late 1930s on his brother-in-law's farm near Epsom, the English public-school officer cadre of the Scots Guards seemed oddly and fascinatingly foreign. Dad spoke with a polite, middle-class Scottish accent, but throughout his life could delivery the accents of broad Doric to recite by heart some of the Aberdeenshire poet 'Hamewith' (Charles Murray) who had known my grandfather, and some of whose recent work my father had learned at school.

> It wasna his wyte he was beddit sae late
> An' him wi' sae muckle to dee,
> He'd the rabbits to feed an' the fulpie to kame
> An' the hens to hish into the ree...

At six-foot, my father had the height for a guardsman, but a pre-war photograph of him stripped to the waist suggests that he did not have the muscles. All the years I knew him he would speak about his 'Scots Guards training' with the same pride and mischief as he recalled 'the poverty of a country home'. In the rural manse, the minister's family had received regular gifts of fresh salmon (too much, my father maintained). Army life, though, was hardly as comfortable. I think my father must have been shocked by some of the military toughness, especially that of his Sergeant Major during training. After the war he would occasionally say 'Yes, Ser'nt Major' as part of his conversation in the family, just as he would polish our shoes religiously, burnishing them to a 'Scots Guards shine'.

Most of the war he spent in England. He was to have been posted abroad sooner, but one of his superior officers, Major Milligan (formerly a master at Eton), so admired his skills as a gardener at Brigade HQ that he arranged for my father to be held back. Quite possibly this saved his life. Of the men my father had known when he first joined the Guards, many had been killed in the retreat from Dunkirk, and only two of his acquaintances survived. Such were the losses that the regiment was reformed and my father, who up to that point had been a bren-gun carrier, now found himself a member of the Sixth Guards Tank Brigade (Scots Guards). One night, just before D-Day, he and his crew were part of a long line of tanks drawn up along a wooded lane in the South of England, waiting for the command to advance. If any tank became disabled, orders were for its crew to push their machine off the road and wait there rather than hold up the whole convoy. By sheer fluke a Luftwaffe plane returning from a raid jettisoned a stray bomb which went right through the hatch of the tank in front of my father's, setting it ablaze and instantly killing the men inside. When the flames had been put out, my father and his colleagues had to move the wreckage off the road and wait behind with their own tank. That was what kept Dad out of the very start of the European invasion, though shortly after the first wave of D-Day landings, his brigade was landed on the Normandy Beaches. He was in Paris around the time of the Liberation and shared in the delight of the local population. He always remembered going to Versailles on a few days' leave and seeing the little row of cottages built for Marie Antoinette near the Petit Trianon. I think its deliberate rustic charm must have reminded him of home.

Not having come to Europe earlier in the war, my father made up for his tardy arrival in the months that followed as he travelled with the Sixth Guards Tank Brigade north through Holland and Germany, eventually as far as the Baltic. He liked the Dutch people especially and for a long time kept in touch with a Dutch family who had been kind to him as he passed through their town. He spoke little about what happened to him at that period, though I think that he must have been involved in the so-called Operation Market Garden, of which the disastrous Arnhem affair was part. I know that he fought in the Battle of Caen and that he was in Cologne shortly after the city had been bombed. Though everyone I knew considered my father to be a gentle man, I assume he must have killed people. I never asked him about that. To have done so would have seemed a betrayal of his love.

In Glasgow in the 1960s my childhood home contained objects brought back as booty in wartime: fine linen table-napkins, model wooden beer-barrels with small, working bronze taps, and, most evocative of all for me as a boy, a pair of black German field-glasses in their tan leather case: 'K.P. Goertz, Bratislava, 6x30 polni kukatko'. I realised later that these must have been made in Czechoslovakia. There was no swastika on them, but, curiously, a logo that appeared to be a small lion rampant. If you peered only through the left-hand lens it was like looking through ordinary binoculars, but if you looked through the right-hand, or through both, you saw a finely-calibrated gunsight.

After the war, which occasioned his only foreign travel, my father wanted absolute respite. He went back to banks in rural Aberdeenshire. He handled Scottish banknotes again. He was close to his father, and to my grandmother. Harbouring the dream of living in a remote cottage not far from Alford at a place called Cattens, possibly he was experiencing what would now be called post-traumatic shock. For some while the Union Bank went along with his wish for quietness and seclusion, but after a time they asked him to move to their London office and it was made clear to him that his answer had to be 'yes'. So my father moved down from rural Aberdeenshire to work in the heart of the City, close to St Paul's Cathedral.

Why they wanted him in London I am not sure. Perhaps his service in the Guards carried with it a certain cachet. He had been a corporal, but had turned down offers of promotion to officer in another, infantry regiment because he thought that would increase his chance of being killed. In the army the officers had commanded his respect, yet also seemed to him amazingly alien. He liked to tell a story about being on a training manoeuvre when, having seen some birds rising above a wood, he had alerted his group to the presence of enemy troops. On being asked by an officer why he thought the enemy was close, he answered, 'Disturbance of wildlife, sir.' The officer commended my father's alertness, but showed also that he considered my father's country *nous* linked him to the despised lower orders. My father heard him mutter under his breath to a fellow officer, 'Name's Crawford... damned poachers!'

In fact, of course, my father was thoroughly respectable. Though a minister's son, he was probably lower middle-class, but certainly he was not Guards-Officer caste. Having passed his exams at the Bank, he was always a teller, eventually Head Teller in a large office, yet never a manager, though for a time he did a manager's job. At work, as in the army, these minute distinctions were regarded as crucial. Even if he maintained respectability all his life, dipping the brim of his hat politely to ladies and gentry, there was something in my father that liked being competently unpromoted, and classed by his superiors as at one with the damned poachers.

In London he must have been on his best behaviour. He admired Anthony Eden, and could cut a dapper, if shy figure. I gather he showed some interest in a girl he knew through the bank there, but she had a club foot which my father felt guilty about disliking. He first met Betty, my mother, around 1950. She had come south from Greenock after an unhappy war-time romance, and wanted to go to London as much as my father had hoped to stay in Aberdeenshire. They were working now in the same office, in Regent Street, off Trafalgar Square. As a bright woman, my mother had received hints of a job in the Bank's Inspector's Department in Glasgow during the war, but this offer had evaporated when male employees came back from the forces. In London she and my father went to see *Coppelia* together. They visited the Festival of Britain in 1951.

When they married, my parents lived in Beckenham, Kent, in a semi-detached house at 129 Merlin Grove. My maternal grandmother moved down to stay with them. They were photographed sitting outside on their wooden garden seat. But my father found the daily commuting on the tube exhausting, and wanted to get back to Scotland. My mother had given up her job by this time, staying at home with her own mother. In 1955 the Union Bank of Scotland amalgamated with the Bank of Scotland and my parents moved north to suburban Cambuslang, near Glasgow, from where my father made a short, daily train journey above ground to his Bank of Scotland office in that city.

When their only child was born in 1959 my father was forty-five and my mother some six years younger. Possibly they had wished, but not expected to have children. My mother suffered from post-natal depression and my father was very frightened by this. He had bought the Cambuslang house from another banker, a Mr Mowat, whose thick-furred Persian cat came along with the transaction. My father simply wrote Mr Mowat a cheque, and Mr Mowat trusted that it would not bounce. My parents lived for forty years in that large, late-Victorian, semi-detached grey sandstone villa; it had a name ('Annieville'), but this was never used. When I was small, its concrete-floored kitchen was changed into one floored with wood. I remember sitting in the doorway of the floorless room, my feet dangling over the edge into the dark depths of the cellar. Also at this time the small maid's bedroom and pantry were amalgamated with the kitchen. The house had several legacies of the days when middle-class families were expected to have domestic servants. It had a serving-hatch, for instance, between what had been the kitchen and the old diningroom which we now called our sittingroom. My parents bought it for £2,500.

Relative to my father's salary, the only income, this was a hefty expenditure. Though he had learned to drive in the army, he let his licence lapse and never quite felt he had the money to run a car. Once I was born, in order to help pay for added home comforts and for the sake of the family, my father gave up smoking. He had smoked a lot in the army, and kept it up after the war. He also maintained that having to wear a metal helmet in wartime had contributed to his going bald on top. I interrogated him about matters like this. I knew that Dad worked in a bank and was very trustworthy. I also knew that when the format of bank stationery changed, he brought home vast quantities of the paper, pads, ledgers and envelopes, stacking and suitcasing them in the cupboard under the stairs. Though I was aware my mother had worked, it was my father whom I saw going out to earn. Very rarely I would actually go and visit him at work behind the heavy mahogany counter of the bank in the magnificent George Square, Glasgow Chief Office, with its great stained-glass dome overhead. For much of his career he had to work on Saturday mornings, and would arrive home at lunchtime with a cardboard box full of bread. One day in his head teller's box he set off an alarm system with his foot by mistake. The whole office was evacuated, the emergency services called to George Square. When they asked who had done this, my father did not confess.

Banking was speeding up now, becoming less personal, and he was aware of the increasing presence of machines. In 1970 the whole British currency changed. We had not long bought a modern record-player at my insistence, and my father brought home a fawn-and-white-sleeved LP with the odd title, 'Decimal Points'. Its seventeen tracks explained the new money in detail; it accompanied a series of programmes on Radio 3. 'This record is to help you cope with the problems of decimal currency… It will also help you with training your staff for D-Day and for the time when you decide that *your* business is to go decimal.' On the record 'role-playing situations' were enacted not entirely convincingly by such people as 'Mrs Joan Laker-Jones of J. Sainsbury' and 'Graham Lawton of Grants of St James's'. My father and I listened to this with fascinated amusement. At first, the new money circulated in tandem with the old – ten-pence coins alongside florins. Suddenly Victoria pennies and three-penny-bits were no longer legal tender. Then the old money disappeared.

Computerisation impacted on my father's work perhaps sooner than in many other professions. For a time I was aware of him and computers working side by side, in a kind of rivalry which allowed my father rather to look down on the machines because of the way they 'made mistakes'. In the early 1970s to help pay my school fees at a grant-maintained school, my father did a lot of overtime. As Head Teller at the Bank of Scotland's chief Glasgow office, he was in charge of calculating salaries for the staff at that branch and others linked to it. This job could be done by computers in Edinburgh, but my father's manager, Mr Thompson, was not keen on losing local control over Glasgow salaries, so he encouraged Dad to do the calculations by hand after hours. He let my father take the work home, and I can remember while I was doing my homework how my mother and father would sit at our solid, square, polished, brown diningroom table with large sheets of figures in front of them, working out exact salaries. My father would take the figures to Mr Thompson in the morning, with a deferential humour that outdid any computer.

By the time he took the option of early retirement in 1974, Dad was very aware that a number of his familiar banking tasks were now handled completely or partially by computer. He was the last person at that branch to calculate the salaries by hand (he used his brain unaided by a pocket calculator). The introduction of Autoteller machines meant that for many transactions there was no need to go into a branch and speak to a human being; everything could be done by a machine embedded in the bank's outside wall. Out of a whimsically maintained piety to my father, rather than out of simple Luddism, I have never used one of these machines. I don't think my father did either.

He would always check his bank statements minutely for mistakes, and taught me to do the same. Once I discovered a large sum that had been credited to me in error. I told the bank, but was scarcely thanked for it. My father was unsurprised that any of this had happened. Having retired when I was in my mid-teens, he offered me the role model of a man far more committed to growing fruit and vegetables in our third-of-an-acre garden than to the technologies of the financial sector. He did buy some tiny amounts of shares in the privatisations of the 1980s, but seemed rather bemused by the process. He trusted National Savings much more than the Big Bang of the stock market. Many of his neighbours now thought of him not so much as a banker, more as a Church Session Clerk or a man whose repertoire extended from swedes to gooseberries, strawberries to brussels sprouts. Occasionally, working in his old clothes, he would be mistaken for an hourly-paid gardener rather than the owner of the semi whose front path he hoed. My father did not teach me much about gardening, seeing that, except as a small boy, I had little passion for it. He did teach me how to save, and, without saying much about it, he brought me up in his religion.

Shortly before my father died, I began to use a computer for the first time. It was in my office at work, and I'm not sure he ever saw it. For over a year after it was installed I didn't do anything with it. Now at least I use it as a word-processor, and summon up one or two databases. Once, when it broke down, a technician came and prized open its casing, revealing drab chips and wiring. But when it is working in its closed body, it has its own sense of animation and activity. What appears on its screen seems tangibly present, yet has almost no being, seems part of a sensation connected both with faith and bereavement. I remember the last time I touched my father's body where he lay collapsed. I knew he was dead, but his face was still warm and stubbly, the essential face of a Dad. The computer after a little while gives off a mild, but unhirsute warmth. It is somehow akin to the machines which replaced my father, yet to which he is linked and I connect him through printing out this. Memories feed the machine, the machine holds memory. The machine too dies, is replaced – not a soul, but a body through which the spirit can be known. My father's lifetime saw the birth of these spirit machines.

On the very morning of Dad's funeral a producer from Radio 3 in Bristol called Tim Dee phoned to ask if I would write a commissioned long poem for broadcast. I said yes, but felt it might be awkward because there could be a weight of obligation forcing me willy-nilly to memorialise my father.

Writing about computers as well was a way of countering the worthy predictability of grief, stopping myself just going through the motions. The computer stuff might seem as up-to-date as my dead father still was to me. Also, when it dated, the computing vocabulary and register might acquire an elegiac patina in tribute to my Dad. Some people might have thought it cold that I should computerise my father, but there was a sense in which doing so was true to the grain of his life, and I did not feel that this excluded a sense of love.

The camera and the telephone were the machines which meant most to him. He was an Instamatic man, taking lots of photographs of places and people he loved. Once he took nine almost identical slides of the beach where we spent our holidays. He would project these and others with the Aldis projector on to a screen in our diningroom. The screen was machine-memory that we would delight in; it was unsurpassed, leery detail. Few people take slides now. That technology has become a memorial. They use videos, camcorders, even digital cameras. I would like to present my father with a digital camera. I did present him with a telephone when he took over the instrument that my wife and I had used in our former home. He spent hours on the telephone, to his brother, to me, to his friends.

When I went in to Edinburgh to record my programme *Spirit Machines* it was a warm, bright September day in 1997, about a month before what would have been my father's eighty-third birthday. I thought about his name. He was called Robert, after his own father, then Alexander, another family name. But he was always known by his second middle name, added on a whim by my grandfather because this new baby had arrived in 1914 on the day of the Battle of Trafalgar. My grandfather sent a telegram, 'Born on this October night/ Another Nelson to the fight.' Most of his life my father's name came to seem more and more anachronistic, linked to a depleting Empire, to what England expected, and to faded or forgotten stars like Nelson Eddy. But at the end, with Nelson Mandela, my father's name became one of the special names of the twentieth century. It was as if an obsolete technology had unexpectedly become again important. An unusual moniker, though, for a white Scot. Its having occurred is like my three-year-old son arriving to interrupt me while I am writing this, suddenly familiar, uncanny, a little unreal.

Rather than turn up early at the BBC studio to record the programme, I went to sit in Princes Street Gardens. There, in the middle of the slow-moving lunchtime crowds, at the head of some steps there stood an impressive mime artist, all in white like a marble statue, except that he occasionally and minutely shifted position with a galvanic, mechanical motion. He was in a white toga, his face covered in white make-up, his fingernails tippexed white. After the recording, which has gone as well as I could have hoped, I remember the little lights in the studio as the sounds were remixed and digitised, my father's names and the names of his familiar places transformed into coded numbers. I go back and sit in the Gardens, relishing the warm autumn heat. I take a notion to go and look at the floral clock. When I was young and my father was at work at the bank, sometimes my mother and I would come through to Edinburgh for a few days' holiday staying with my Aunt Maimie in Morningside. We'd go to Princes Street Gardens to look at the floral clock. I stood in front at the stone balustrade with other children, waiting for the hands of the clock that were wood and metal machinery covered with plants to come round to the hour, or even the quarter hour. A mechanical bird would come out of a real bush next to the clock. We would try to photograph it for the instant it was visible. The clock was in a corner of the Gardens close to the Scott Monument. Each year it would be replanted in a slightly different design with flowers spelling words – the name of a charity, the 1970 Commonwealth Games, the Edinburgh International Festival. I haven't seen it for a while, and now I can't find it. Where is the floral clock? Later, I'll be told I was just looking in the wrong place, but on that day I'm sure I am standing where it used to be, beside the flight of stone steps to the lower gardens. The clock has gone completely, and the bush with the bird in it. The hands, the hours and minutes are all away. There's just a bare plot. Still, looking down at the soil, I am at the edge of a shifting crowd of pedestrians. It is as if for a moment I had sidestepped out of time.

Allan Crosbie

SIGNING

the language of touch, the speechless
vocabulary of hands.

From 'Request' by Norman MacCaig

From your signing class you show me *giraffe* and *camel*.
You show me *I want* and *I do not want*.
I want to ask for *give* and *take*, which you know well,
your hands sweeping like swallows,
but I'm scared you'll just give me the usual two fingers,
a quick stab upwards with the 'V'
and a smirk that says everything.

My hands speak their own language,
whispering the names of unknown animals
and strange desires on the sounding board of your body.
But you correct my fingers' grammar,
making my hands clumsy as hammers
as you fall asleep to dream of words sculpted in the air
until I wake you, signing *water* on your face.

Anna Crowe

CLOSE

They are still here, the walled-up dead.
Their stifled cries, a tightness in the chest;
blood pounding in our ears,
their fists on doors.

This slum is under the street.
Above us, twelve or thirteen floors
rise like Babel into Edinburgh's night:
chandeliers, mirrors, portraits,
Scotland's history, sins of the fathers.

This was once a butcher's.
When they unblocked the close,
moist, damp air blew in,
and faded stains in the plaster
freshened and bloomed.

Those who came on Egypt's royal dead
uncorked a stoppered air,
catching a breath of spikenard or myrrh
before it sighed and was gone.

Stumbling over cobbles, our feet disturb
a whiff of byre – cow-dung
and sweetly, faintly, hay;
round the next corner,
brief, fragrant, unmistakable,
baking bread.

Anne Donovan

TESTING

I don't bother reading the instructions now. Just pee on the absorbent cotton wool stuff, counting ten seconds, then lay the white tube on the edge of the bath, watching the liquid seep through the plastic windows till the first line forms. *This indicates the test is complete and has worked correctly.* No line in the other window. Not pregnant. Again.

I sit on the toilet for a bit longer, watching the ghost lines, the might-have-been babies in the white plastic frame. It's not just my imagination, you really can see faint vertical lines, paler than the white – it must be something to do with how the test works.

The line in the Boots test is blue. I don't like that as much as the pink of the other brand. Pink is more welcoming, you're more likely to be pregnant with a pink test, and even when it's negative it's more reassuring, more *maybe-next-time, try again* than the unrelenting cold blue NO. The Boots test is a pound cheaper though, and these tests are dear. If my cycle would get back to normal I'd know where I stand. I know it's mad doing this every few days but I can't help it.

These tests are brilliant. Three minutes any time of day. 99% accurate. And they look so neat, like a designer pen, slim-line with a cap to cover the bit you pee on. You could even use the Boots one as a pen because the absorbent bit is open, you could dip it into ink and paint with it, Japanese brush strokes, sparse, clean.

The blood soaked through three pairs of knickers and as many super-absorbent sanitary towels in an hour. I had to send him home for more. When I went to get washed I kept dripping over the floor of the hospital toilet, one of those greeny-grey speckled floors with shiny bits through it. So red the blood. Primary red, pure with no other colour mixed in it.

The pregnancy tests are in the bottom shelf of the middle aisle at the back end of the shop, thoughtfully placed next to the contraceptives. I go in the right-hand door of the shop, picking up some toothpaste and dental floss en route, linger at the Bach Flower Remedies, checking to see if there's anyone I

know about, swiftly pick up the test and walk purposefully to
the till, avoiding the one with the young man. My till receipt
tells me that at 12.50 I was served by Louise and bought BTS
F/F SENS 75ML and ORAL B ULTRAFLOSS but where it
should say BTS PREG TEST the computer has written
CHEMIST GOODS. Is this in case your mother goes through
your purse checking your receipts or because you bought a
sandwich along with your test and don't want your boss to
know when he checks your expenses claim? Maybe it's to stop
you using your receipt to claim a refund if you're not satisfied
with the test.

*Look here, this test's no use. It should be giving me a pos-
itive result.*

I'm afraid we can't guarantee a positive result, madam.

*Yes but it must be positive, we've been having sex nearly
every day and I haven't had a period since…*

*Let me see your receipt. Oh no, madam, this isn't a receipt
for a pregnancy test, it says CHEMIST GOODS.*

The first test I ever did was positive. I nipped out to buy it
during my break on Monday morning, the day I'd missed my
period, and was so excited I rushed to the toilet at work, sitting
in the cold, old-fashioned cubicle, unwrapping the cellophane,
reading the instructions carefully. It said wait three minutes but
as the liquid flowed through, the two pink lines appeared right
away, a matching smile seeping over my face. *A positive result
line should be visible for twenty-four hours.* The smile stayed
on my face for at least that long.

I did another one the following week just to be sure before
I went to the doctor's. I didn't feel any different, didn't know
what to feel anyway. Later came that uncomfortable heaviness
in my breasts, as if the skin was stretching, that feeling I keep
imagining now. Like a cow waiting to be milked. The second
test was positive yet I still couldn't quite believe it. Pregnant
first time. Surely it couldn't be that easy.

I have a photo of the scan they did at six weeks; the baby is
just a blurred shape but they could tell it was alive then by the
heartbeat which shows like a pulse of light. I always thought
the womb was shaped like an upside-down pear, that's what
they tell you in the books, but it isn't. In the photo it's the shape
of a heart. A baby in the womb is a heartbeat inside a heart.

I'm sorry, I can't find a heartbeat.

I knew there was something wrong. It was the way she moved the probe, slithering around on the jelly. There was a hesitancy, like someone learning to dance who keeps stopping to get back into a lost rhythm.

At this stage the foetus should be the size for ten weeks and it's only eight. Something must have happened two weeks ago and it just stopped growing. I'm sorry.

Her hand on my left arm. I look at the ceiling. His hand on my right arm.

I'm very sorry. I'll go and get someone to speak to you.

It was Hogmanay and the scanning department had shut down for the holiday so we were led through a dark corridor past locked doors to a cold office. Muffled in layers of winter clothes, I could not stop shivering. They were kind. I walked home through the fading light, carrying a dead baby inside me. On New Year's Day I returned and gave birth.

I buy the pink test this time, in Boots in the St Enoch Centre so I don't have to be furtive like I am in my local shop, and can even chat about the weather to the woman at the till. I'm becoming more blase about it anyway, buying the test on its own, not putting it in the bottom of a basket under a pile of deodorants and cough sweets. When I get home, though, I hide it in the top drawer under my knickers. He doesn't know I keep testing. I do it secretly, like an addict, when he's out or before he gets up in the morning, running the shower while I wait for the result. I don't tell him about the dreams either.

I was trying to put the baby into a cassette case, having separated the two halves and taken out the tape. The baby fitted into the bottom half because it was tiny and curled up into a foetal position but when I put the top half of the case on it wouldn't shut properly. I pressed the two halves of the case together and looked at the baby through the smoked plastic glass. Then its mother came through the door and I looked at her, suddenly shocked, realising that I had killed the baby and would have to tell her.

It is five o'clock in the morning and the cold white bathroom glares at me. Tuesday. I last did one three days ago. I sit on the toilet, take the test out of my dressing gown pocket, unwrap the cellophane, hold the white plastic tube under me and pee, counting the seconds.

Bill Duncan

MAIR BAATHER

Hell o a stramash up at The Puffin last week.

Mair baather?

Blood Transfusion Unit, Mobile Cardiac Arrest, twa Police Vans, Casualty Department an Intensive Care Ward aa involved.

Bad baather. Wha wiz aa there?

Wullie The Tortoise, The Maist Ignorant Man In The World, Captain Ahab, The Weasel, The Submarine Commander, Muscleman, The Creator, Barkin Doaggie, The One-Man-Crowd, The Mathematician, an Big Norrie.

Weemin involved?

Men **an** weemin.

Bad combination. Ye can hae men or weemin. Canna hae baith.

Correct. Ane or the ither. Specially when drink an Big Norrie's involved.

That the same lad wiz involved in some baather wi a Frozen Chicken an a Russian Hat?

Ehh. Norrie took tae wearin a big black furry Cossack hat in the winter. He wid shoplift occasionally in Safeway's an this time he's wearin the hat an decides tae tak a frozen chicken. Braa big hat. Naebody's lookin. Stuffs the chicken intae the hat an puts the hat back on. Nae problem til he got tae the checkout wi a half bottle o Navy Rum an a 5 litre tin o Vinyl Matt Brilliant White Emulsion.

Under the hat?

Dinnae be stupit. Setterday efternain wi a big queue at the checkout an the heatin turned up fur the caald spell an the chicken starts tae thaw wi the waater dreepin doon Norrie's forehead an nose. Young Assistant Manager wi the waistcoat, bow-tie an concerned expression thinks Norrie's haein a wee turn an he's straight ower wi 'Can I help you, Sir? You appear to be in some distress. May I assist in any way?' Shop's got a new Customer Care Scheme in place wi Accelerated Promotion Opportunities fur any member o staff that customers say nice things tae Heid Office aboot on the Customer Care Freephone Helpline.

Well Big Norrie's no sae concerned wi The Assistant Non-Food Manager's career prospects as he is aboot avoidin arrest again.

'Naw – it's awright. It's jist a bit on the waarm side in the store the day.'

'Perhaps if you were to remove the hat, sir...'

'Naw! Yer awright, son!' an flees the store wi one hand on the Russian Hat an the ither shovin puzzled customers oot the road. So that wiz a few weeks ago an Norrie's shoppin in Asda noo.

Last week's baather worse?

Far worse. Crowd o them up at The Puffin. Men an weemin – Big Norrie an Marilyn, an The Weasel on his ain – ye'll ken he split up wi Avril efter the Giant Man-Eatin Pacific Squid fiasco, an has a wee flat doon fae the pub. Noo Big Norrie kens Weasel an Marilyn go back a lang time an Norrie's edgy aboot this because Weasel reminds him aboot it whenever there's a certain amount been drunk. A risky caper, if ye ask me. Anywey, Norrie's in the Public Bar fur the Knife-Throwin Semi-finals an by the time he gets back tae the Lounge, Marilyn's gone. An nae sign o The Weasel. Beh this time Norrie's seein aa kind o things in his heid an roarin about sortin that bastard oot once an fur aa an he staggers oot the front door even though The Submarine Commander an The One-Man-Crowd are daein their best tae restrain him. But no. Big Norrie heads straight fur The Weasel's flat. So he's doon the road an aa fired up an the next thing he's trehin tae batter the door doon, chargin at it ower and ower baalin aboot cheatin couple o bastards an swingin fur thum baith. However, the door steys put an, wi a bit o a crowd startin tae gether beh this time, Big Norrie flings himsel through the livin room windae in a riot o gless, roarin an blood. An aald lad's sittin waatchin the highlights o Herts versus Dunfermline on Sportscene wi the volume turned up fuhl an beh this time Norrie's in a bad wey, craalin aboot the flair, moanin, semi-conscious an lossin blood fest while the aald lad's in a state o severe shock. Wrang hoose. The Weasel's in his bed in the next tenement an Marilyn's gone hame lang ago.

Some kerry on, right enough.

Ehh. Big Norrie's a gentleman maist o the time but gets edgy wi the drink. His twa young lads the same, mind. Rab an Davie fight ane anither maist weekends an Big Norrie has a fight wi wan or the ither o them at least wance a month. Hell o a baather when Davie turned up wearin the Rangers strip, an Rab wi the Celtic strip on fur the Old Firm match on Sky.

Mind you, some say Rab wid start a fight in an empty room an Davie wid hae a square go wi his ain shadow.

That's Big Norrie ower there. Big smilin fella wi the neck brace on an the airm in a sling. That's the twa young lads. Seeminly Norrie tends tae dae that kind o thing mibbee fower or fehv times a year. Looks like Big Norrie's gone ower far though.

Colleagues in the Philosophy Department are insistin on The Anger Management Course this time.

Gerrie Fellows

From *The Separations*

THE GLORY SIGNS

Beyond its crested name Bannockburn's mown grass
is spick and span and nothing like
the morass of the carse the enemy blundered into
mown down by arrow tips and the spikes of lances
Duplicity of signs: to the intruder they signalled
battle lines, flat ground   beneath the outward sign
a whisper   *between our mountains and our firths*
the suck of our carses   to the visitor they signal
Scotland the Brave   a tableau of chain-mailed soldiers
a swagged stallion on a null expanse with plinth
and flagpole   the sign of a great victory
and only the Bruce, blind with armour   high enough
to eye the battlefield where the A91 hurls itself
like a crazed charger over the meadow flowers
The real battle was underground in the labyrinthine
measures of coal   earth's black body of burning
which season by season fell to the hands of serfs
before it fell to the hands of others
The real minefield is the labyrinth of history
where miners on their last shift encounter the dead
of empire   from glory to glory Scotland's heritage:
a home fire, a furnace, a wee bitty cloth
like a flag the flower of Scotland wore in battle
in the dusty heights of the great game
a sign   and beneath the sign   a whisper

ERASING THE TAPE

Aviemore: she thinks she knows the place   keeps
driving past the car park pizza joint brute hotel
keeps driving past her own peripheral vision
gone in the blink of a Polaroid the fields of famine
the nettle tops and mugwort of a bad year, king's evil
all he'd fled from to become his own fantastical idea
She keeps driving   she will erase history as if
it were a taped forest of ancient pines   she will
rewind the machine   be clear of voices and dreams
She drives over the ghostliest refraction of a sound
and he catches her in his mind   for he is a memory
rooted in the dark like a child smothered face down
among tree roots in peat, ineradicable   refusing
to become a bland visage among the idling crowds
cursed, he will uncover all he fled from
Beyond the shutter's click he will take the wheel
he will drive her with a shiver of hands
past barked stumps, pine dark water   to the screes
of what she thinks she knows   an eerie
and forlorn spaciousness   He wants to show her
This is my country   these are the hobgoblin rotors
wire coiled at the back of a wheelhouse   labour
not love, its mutilations   the strange towers
the wind sings through, the mournful crucifixes

LANDSCAPE WITH SIGNS

A tourist strolls between mossed dykes in search
of the Ettrick Shepherd   (It is the ninth month
the beginning of autumn, the road deep with mud)
In memory of his wife   (the waters swollen)
he has come to trace the forebear of his children
(There was a want of bridges   the waters broken
For many hours he was obstructed on his journey)
At first he'd believed the road would transport him
as we had unpeeled it into the twentieth century
so it would unreel us into an ancestral stratum
His car is parked on a grassy verge   he saunters
away from the lane uphill into focal distance
He knows he is venturing into the past   that this
is what it meant   the unnavigable tracks, the want
of bridges   for he is a man who has envisaged
flyovers, underpasses, highways   the concrete signs
by which we've chosen to possess our time
A sheep fold holds the lie of a paddock
a part of the body of earth as a road is   camberred
topsoil overlies its stern elemental
This is what earth is   is what he makes the future of
the past and present tense   of prose
impervious Ettrick traversed by roads
of ballads   of bewitched and footless journeys

Jim Ferguson

OLIVES

when i had cash
and duly purchased
olives stuffed
with pimentos

the olives were mouths
the pimentos tongues
and they spake unto me thus

'look out to your future
save your pennies
for one day soon
ye shall be skint'

Moria Forsyth

GOOD ADVICE

Catriona jigs behind me, out of sight, but I can't turn round
just yet. The water boils, and I tip in the rice.
'Look,' she says. '*Look*, Mum. What d'ya think? Up?' I half
turn, and she sweeps blonde hair high on her head, then lets it
fall in a swift curtain. 'Or down?'
'Lovely,' I say, turning the heat down, checking the oven.
I'm in a hurry, trying to get some nourishing food into her
before she eats the whole packet of chocolate digestives. 'Leave
those, Catriona, the tea's nearly ready.'
'Well, I'm starving, you're really *late*.'
'We're busy just now. Sorry.'
'Why d'you have to work late, anyhow, can't somebody
else do it?'
'No, so don't go on about it. I do my best.' The rice boils
over: there are starchy streaks down the side of the pan, and a
smell of burning. 'I don't see why you couldn't make tea some-
times – that would speed things up.'
'I can't cook.'
'You could learn.'
'You teach me, then.'
We've been round this circle before. If I haven't time to
come home and cook interesting meals, how can I find time to
teach her how to do it?
Eventually, we sit down and she wolfs food in silence for a
few minutes, then says with her mouth full,
'You never said about my hair. What you think suits me
best.'
'Don't talk while you're eating.'
'Sorry.' But she's still chewing. She talks, I talk. But we're
each listening to our own thoughts.
'So is that all right?' she says, and I wake up to the fact
that she wants something.
'What?'
'Mu-um!' She sighs, setting down her fork. 'I'm full up.'
'You haven't eaten your veg.'
'I said – I'm full.'
'I told you not to eat all those biscuits.'
'I was hungry, though.'

'Oh don't start that again. What were you asking me?'

'Will you give Emma and Claire a lift to the disco?'

'Tonight?'

'Yes of course, tonight. Wouldn't be much point any other night, would there?'

'Don't. Don't speak to me like that. We're picking them up on the way, is that it?'

'Yeah, and then I'm goin back to Claire's after, could you take us back there after, and bring my sleepin bag an stuff?'

'Yes, all right.' I'm too tired to protest, and after all, what else am I going to do with my Friday night? Watch Gardeners' World, drink the one whisky I allow myself. John hasn't phoned, and I'm certainly not going to call him.

'And mind,' Catriona says, as we get in the car, 'when you come and collect us, you park on the other side of the road, and you don't get out of the car, just wait for us to come up. OK?'

'Right,' I say, 'your Majesty.' But this goes over her head with its new washed fall of hair. Fortunately, the copper rinse that dyed three towels pink and left a seemingly indelible stain on the bathroom wall, has almost gone. And she is so pretty, in her tight cotton top and new white jeans, that my heart skips with love, leaps over irritation, soothes my loneliness.

We draw up outside Claire's house, and she jumps out to go and ring the doorbell. Claire has been waiting, in black trousers and equally tiny tee-shirt, and they meet at the gate. They get in the back together, talking.

Later, at home, I watch Gardeners' World, write down the name of a new delphinium, which I shall probably never buy, and wait for the phone to ring. When it does, it's my mother.

'I thought you might be out tonight,' she says, 'with that man – what did you say his name was?' If she thought I might be out, why did she phone? And she knows very well what his name is. But she can't keep the pity from her voice, because she is seventy-two, and has had the same husband for fifty years, and I am forty-two, and mine left me. I don't think she holds out much hope for me getting another one.

'No,' I tell her, 'I have to fetch Catriona and her pals from their disco at half past ten.'

'Oh my, a disco, at her age.'

'It's only in the village hall, and no-body over fifteen goes.' I don't tell her what Catriona told me – that a lot of the boys are drunk, that they've been knocking back cans of export in the car park before going in. I don't tell her about John either, and I know she won't probe. She is very delicate in her sensibilities, my mother. We talk instead about my father's arthritis and the new delphinium.

'My geraniums have done so well this year,' she says. 'Half way through October, and they're still covered in blooms. What about those cuttings I gave you? Did they come away all right?'

'Some of them... the greenfly got to them, though, I wasn't quick enough with my spray.'

'It's not too late,' she reassures me. 'Just cut them hard back – they'll do fine next spring, dear.'

By the time this conversation ends, it's almost time for me to go for the girls, so temptation has been removed. My mother has done me a favour: there's no time to ring John.

When the girls appear, what strikes me is how like all the other girls they are: leggy and lean with shiny hair and tight clothes. I push open the passenger door and they tip up the seat to clamber into the back together, all three crammed tight. The car is filled with three kinds of cheap scent, and sweat, and the reek of salt and vinegar crisps.

'Put it off, Mum, people might hear it.'

'What?'

'I bet it's Runrig. Is it Mum, is it Runrig? That's all she listens to, she's mad, my Mum. Put on the radio instead.'

Catriona's on a high; they all are. I open the window to disperse the various smells, and drive off. But I keep my music, though I can hardly hear it for their young raised voices, the crackle of crisp packets. John gave me this tape.

'Well,' I ask them, 'how did it go?'

'Clare get dumped but she got off with Fraser instead, didn't you Claire? So she's not bothered about Jamie, he went off with this girl in 3R, she's so dumb, isn't she? And Emma nearly got off with this boy from Marybank, he's Ian Sutherland's cousin, but he's only here because he goes to an English school and it's their half term, so there was no point really.'

'He was nice, though,' Emma sighed. 'He had this really cool tea-shirt, Calvin Kline, grey and black.'

'And what about you, Catriona?' It must be all right. And it is. Claire and Emma chant together:

'Ooh – ooh – Catriona got off with Spee-eed, Catriona got off with Spee-eed!'

They all laugh helplessly and tear open another packet of crisps.

'What about you, then, Mum? Did John phone?'

I should say, don't be cheeky, or none of your business. It's not supposed to be this way round. But a week ago she came into my bedroom to borrow tights, and found me crying, so low I couldn't think what to tell her except the truth.

'He's a crap boyfriend, Mum,' she said. 'Just dump him. You could easy get somebody better, you're really pretty for your age. And he's ugly, don't you think?' I started to laugh, in spite of the tears, and feeling so terrible. Catriona fetched the box of tissues and sat beside me on the bed till I dried up a bit. Then, seeing an opportunity, she started whittling away again at my resistance to spending £33 on an Aberdeen football shirt.

Now, all I can say in reply to her frank enquiry is 'No, Granny rang, I was on the line to her for over half an hour.'

'So he could have phoned, eh? That's good, it's good not to be available when a guy phones, it said that in *Just 17* this month.'

I realise suddenly that what she is trying to do is include me. Not mock, or be impertinent, or show me up in front of her friends. Include me. In the back of my small car, cosily crushed together, they are going over the important things that have happened. And Catriona, who orders me around with peremptory rudeness, takes me for granted, goes her own way, is trying to make me part of it.

'Well,' I say, 'it doesn't matter anyway. I've decided to dump him.'

In the back, they all cheer, so I turn up Runrig full blast, and they shriek at me to switch it off.

When I get home, I'm alone. They have gone to Claire's to talk half the night and sleep all next morning, and come home grumpy in time for lunch. The house is silent and dark, but before I switch on the light, I see the red button flashing on the answerphone.

'I've been trying to get you all night – no reply, then engaged, now the answerphone. Give me a ring when you get in. I'll still be up and about. Bye.'

I stand by the phone while the tape whirrs back, clicks off. And I wonder,

What would Catriona do?

Pete Fortune

A DEATH IN THE FAMILY

My brother is going to die. Nobody knows for sure when this will happen (how can they?) but the consultant dealing with his case reckons somewhere between a couple of months and a year. This is what he told me, the end of August 1997:

'We have the results of John's tests, and the news is not great. He has a tumour on his left lung, and it has attached itself to surrounding bone structure. This is what is causing him such pain in his shoulder and back. A couple of ribs are actually cracked, and we hope that radiotherapy will reduce the size of the tumour, and alleviate the pain to an extent. That's all we can hope to achieve though. Nobody's talking about a cure here, I have to emphasise that. I'm afraid the outlook is pretty grim.'

He went on to tell me that a bone scan had also revealed what he referred to as a cluster of hot spots elsewhere, mainly in John's left leg and arm. It seemed that cancerous growths were on the verge of erupting there too. I'd been expecting bad news because John had looked really unwell for some time, but all the same, it was still a shock hearing it confirmed.

'How long do you think he has?' I asked.

'Difficult to say,' he replied. 'The sort of tumour he has tends to be slow-growing, but if it moves into the centre of his chest I'd expect him to deteriorate rapidly. It could be a couple of months, it could be a year. The quality of life remaining is what concerns us now though. I can assure you, we will see to it that he is kept as comfortable as possible.'

Actually, my brother died twelve years ago, but they got him going again. He fell down a flight of stairs and lay undiscovered for around eight hours. He developed a blood clot on the brain, and by the time someone discovered him he was in a pretty bad way. I got a phone call to say he was in hospital suffering from concussion.

When I arrived at the hospital they gave it to me straight. 'We need to transfer him to the Southern General in Glasgow for specialist treatment, or he's going to die. Trouble is, if we attempt to move him right now, there's every likelihood that he'll die.' I said to move him, and they did. And he lived.

John was in a coma for a couple of weeks, and in hospital

for months, but live he did, despite the fact that his heart actually stopped beating a couple of times. He emerged a different person though, 'head injured' the euphemism, brain damaged the fact of the matter. His basic intelligence was intact, but the most disturbing thing was the fairly profound personality change which had taken place. At times it was as if another human being had been implanted in my brother's body. He seemed generally 'odd' too. It sounds cruel but it's true because I heard people say so – *he's kind of odd now.*

But he eventually returned to the community, living alone in his flat (he'd gone through a divorce just before his accident) and generally muddling along. He got by, just. I can see in retrospect that he needed more support than he ever got – especially from me – but to indulge in an outpouring of guilt would be an attempt to exorcise it, and I'm not about to go into that.

So my brother had a go at dying once before, and now here he is again. This time the consultant seems pretty certain he *will* die – just a matter of when. Never once did the consultant mention the word cancer to me – tumour was the most direct reference he made, along with a host of other terms which later had me fumbling through the dictionary. Maybe if he'd used the word cancer to John, the message might have got through. He said he'd told my brother he had a tumour and that they were going to attempt treating it with radiotherapy – they'd just have to wait and see. He'd left it at that, hoping the rest would be deduced.

John told me he had a tumour, but that there was nothing to worry about, it was benign and they were going to zap it with radiotherapy. The worst that could happen was that he'd maybe go bald. He said being bald at 52 was no big deal. He said things could have turned out a whole lot worse. He smiled as he said so.

I spoke to his GP about the situation. I'd been in recent contact with him, because we were both concerned about John's living conditions. His head injury had left him negligent when it came to hygiene issues, and the mess he'd been living in amounted to self-neglect. I told the GP about my brother's confusion regarding his diagnosis and prognosis. I presumed it was down to his head injury. The doc reckoned not necessarily so, said it could be a classic case of denial. He saw it all the time, said many terminally ill people just put the shutters up when told of their fate, just completely blocked out the facts and constructed an alternative reality. He said it was best I just go along with it, let John dictate the pace. 'Who are you?' he said, 'to deny him his denial?'

So I do go along with it, wondering each visiting hour how things will be. There's friends and relatives visiting who John hasn't seen in a long time – I wonder if that doesn't tell him that something serious is going on. There's the chance too that one of them will be verbally explicit, confront him with his fate. Sometimes too I wonder if he *does* fully understand, but is maybe trying to protect me, and I'm going along with the pretence, trying to protect him. A weird kind of cat and mouse game, perhaps?

Once the news had properly sunk in I became briefly obsessed with the whole business of cancer, became convinced for a while that I had it – *that everyone I loved had it*. Then I grew curious and sought out the text books in the library. I learned some really gory things about cancer, but managed to divorce those terrible things from the illness my brother was suffering. Maybe I was into a kind of denial too?

Anyway, I learned that quite often a tumour will resemble the host body. That is to say, a kidney tumour may well be made up of – in effect – another kidney, gone kind of haywire. Or the tumour may *not* resemble the host body at all. Tumours for example can grow hair, or even have teeth. Having teeth seemed the worst thing of all, the thought of this thing growing inside you – *with teeth*. It seemed so symbolically apt in a very macabre sort of way. It made me realise why medical people have to so often resort to euphemism.

I forced myself away from the text books. Morbid. Besides, there was practical issues to deal with. John hasn't worked since his head injury, had been on jobseeker's allowance. I don't think he could ever have held down a job again, but that's academic. He's certainly not fit to work now, so he had to be transferred across to another benefit, to incapacity benefit. I handled all the paperwork for him, four books – not forms – *books of forms*, all of which asked for pretty much the same information. My head still reeling from the fact that my brother's dying, but the state demands that all this paperwork be dealt with, and at the end of the day he'll still receive exactly the same amount of (meagre) money in benefits.

A week after I'd filled in all those forms, a matching set was sent to the hospital for John to fill in. No one knows what happened to the ones I filled in, and nobody knows either when he's likely to receive any money. Nobody seems to really care. All the young women I've dealt with seem polite and very charming, but quite unable to supply anything approaching useful information. The caring state under New Labour.

The state's going to have to play another role too. Once released from hospital, John's going to need home help, meals on wheels, nurses to call in and check on medication, etc., all that kind of business. A medical social worker is organising this side of things, and I'm working in liaison with her. At times it seems as if my whole life has been hijacked to help organise what's left of my brother's. I'm not complaining about this, how can I? If that's not what brothers are for, then what exactly is it they're meant to be for?

So as I write he's still in hospital, and we're still waiting for the care package to fall into place. Last night when I visited him he was talking again about what he was going to do once he was better. I can never look him in the eye when he talks that way, like the whole pretence has stripped away any honesty that exists in our relationship. But he's entitled to his denial. It's maybe the last thing he has. But all the same, I think, he must know what's going on. Somewhere, deep deep down, he *must* know. Or is the human psyche really capable of such a massive deception? Will he just grow weaker and weaker, all muddled up with drugs and just slip away? Without properly knowing?

He phoned me there. Just as I finished typing that paragraph the phone rang and it was him phoning from hospital. From the portable public phone they can wheel alongside your bed, where sometimes the nurses just stand and listen to the conversation. They do – some of them – I've seen them. Anyway he phoned, and he needs me to bring some matches or a lighter when I visit later on. He's clean out and he's desperate. He's in hospital dying of lung cancer and still he smokes about forty a day. Two lethal cuts of hand-rolling stuff – which he mixes together – and then puff puff puffs in this smelly little smoking room he has access to. What the hell. What's the point in him stopping now? But anyway he phoned and that's good because it's like he gets to put in a live appearance here. Yes, that's good. That's defiance for you.

I appreciate defiance. Death's been big news of late, the death of someone we were encouraged to see as defiant. While my brother's illness was revealing itself up there on the Bankend Road, Diana, Princess of Wales – scourge of the royal establishment – got herself killed. By all accounts the driver was well over the legal alcohol limit, as well as having a cocktail of drugs flowing through him, and on top of it all it seems he was doing well over the ton. Response? Blame the boys on the scooters. I suppose such a ridiculous response amounts to a kind of defiance too.

The mass hysteria her death generated I would have found hard enough to take at any time, but for it to coincide with my brother's news was lousy timing. Sometimes it made me angry, and I wanted to go and kick the bunches of flowers dumped around Queensberry Square. Chase away all the silly old women reading the messages on the cards. But the whole thing was weird. Really, really weird. It was like grief manifesting itself as a human *desire*. All those people seemed to *want* something to be sad about. I can only figure they must have uneventful lives. Diana's seemed a kind of glamorous death, with loads of romantic ingredients mixed in. Maybe that was the attraction. But real death's not like that.

I see real death almost every night I'm up at the hospital visiting my brother. Real death's catching a glimpse of a little old man all hunched up in bed, face invisible beneath an oxygen mask, scrawny little rib cage going ten to the dozen. Real death's seeing his wife sitting bearing witness to it all, his grown-up sons not knowing what to do or say, of maybe wanting to – but being too embarrassed to – put their arms around their old mum.

Real death is my brother waiting to happen. Real death is why I'm writing this: I suppose it might seem to some people a kind of brutal and cold-hearted response to my brother's death. Or at least the death I'm told can't be far away. But I don't know why I'm writing about it. I'm a writer of sorts, and I suppose it's what writers do. We write about things. It's probably never done any writer – or anybody in the world – much good, even if we like to kid ourselves on from time to time that it does. *It's art. Others might find benefit. There is a universal truth.* All that kind of nonsense. But I don't know what the hell I can do and so I find myself doing this, and feeling tacky and manipulative in the process.

And so to the end – sometimes in my stories I have difficulties with endings. This piece has a natural ending – still to come – and no one knows for sure when that will be. Being a fiction writer, I know that some people speculate as to what's real and what's made up in my stories. No one need do that with this piece. This is the real thing – and it's grim.

This is what they mean by dirty realism.

John Fortune died on 30th October 1997
R.I.P. Brother

R. Friel

SITCOM

1. Fiat

Lowering a mug of tea
Onto my MFI work surface,
I pulled out a sheaf of half-baked
Poems on a biblical theme, brought my Fineline
To bear on a draft of *Apocrypha*, and triggered
A rattling explosion under my window.

The cablemen had come
To bury 40 channels in our pavement
(...*in our hearts*).

I strode outside
To a man with headphones
Bopping a pneumatic:
'I'M TRYING TO WRITE!'
                              'What?' he shouted,
Pulling off headphones.
'I said, it's turned out bright!' He looked at me
As if to say, *what a prick*. 'You'll have to move that,'
He continued, nodding towards
Our Cinquecento. 'With pleasure,' I heard myself
Saying, my stomach for a fight passing
Into the realms of myth.

When we returned, later that day,
A fresh black scar ran the length of the cul-de-sac,
Unmoved cars coated in dust.
Unlike our gleaming chrome:

Fiat Lux.

2. Victor

On the second day,
Their legacy was clear:
Lines severed, trees cut off
From sustaining darkness,
Distressed privets.

When the rep gave in
And came round
Victor (aka Richard Wilson,
b. Greenock)
Threw up his sash window
And delivered a *Suburbi et Orbi*
On the new menace
Facing the Close:
'You know what you can do
With your bloody cable television
Don't you, matey!'
                              Which was fine
Until the window slipped
And guillotined
The voice of the people,
The rock on which
Our dour resistance is built.

3. Eulogy

From behind a tree,
In neck brace
And corded dressing-gown,
He scanned the little scrum of mourners,
Catching snippets of the vicar's ponderous eulogy
Not smothered by the blustery day:
'Our dear departed brother, Victor...
patron of lost causes... caustic defender
of the unconventional...
cut off tragically in his prime.'
His jaw was lowering like the hydraulics
On a Pickford's removal van
When he spotted his own poor wife
Dropping in a rose, steered away rather too fondly
By Widget, the car dealer from next door.
'Right!' said Victor, scuffing through the headstones
In carpet slippers. 'What's the meaning of this?'
        'Not *now*, Victor,' she pleaded,
And went her lugubrious way; then stopped
Stock still, and swooned round
Into a gaping grave.
Pandemonium.

Laughter

Until she saw
The circle of leaning-in faces part
And there he was, the light behind him,
Reaching out a hand
To lift her out of there
And hold her like there was no tomorrow.

Iain Galbraith

DIVAN

in memoriam Isabella MacAllister & James Galbraith,

married 5.11.1819, Bonhill

A vista wrought for a royal jaunt would likely sleek
Our Lord Blantyre who henceforth saw his pleasure's
     commerce
Entered to the darkening glister of Venice and Delft –
Sequestrated promise downset in Claudian willows,
An umbrous Bowling canal. Dumbarton Rock's the smirr

Of ages fast in erd and stane, a warrandice
To steamboats coursing for the grand emporium's heart.
On my lap's a westward view from Milton or Dalnottar,
Clouds ablaze like fiery garments over the Clyde.
The mind's eye flees, reaches, squints, hurries

Back with dyers, printers, mills, the blackened grass:
A weavers' road that hurtles through the mutable estates
Where wick and virtue flare to the music of fife,
The torchlit scintill of three hundred shattered
     panes.
The late train to Tarbet gently halts and hums –

The voice regrets the hindrance left across the rails
(Two boys, one me, later reported
Scaling the embankment with a bedstead).
Troubled I return to my po-faced sheep – Arcadia
     complete
with a penny wedding, tittling billie, the guidwife
     in her mutch.

Valerie Gillies

BASKING ADDERS

a tailed sonnet

After rain, out come the adders
Sun-basking on a bank of earth

Below the hill they give their name to, Nathro,
We see great snakes dazzle the turf.

Brown mother-adder, short head and tail,
One long muscle with a copper eye

Glides forward, propelled by belly-scales
Each scale an oar to row her by

And on the sunny slope her viper-brood
The young of one year old entwine and coil

In running knots and loop-the-loop
Beaded bronze wire soldered in spirals.

Sunlight twists in their skin, little stick-pins
Hold their spectators. They are transfixing

Us to adderstanes. We stand as close as we can,
The lucky amulet punctured by the fang.

Note
Adderstane: a small prehistoric stone or bead,
supposed to be perforated by the stings of
adders, and later used as a talisman. Probably
a weight for fishing line in neolithic times.

George Gunn

OTTERS

A head appears in the rivermouth
like a small black whiskered stone
then another, reclining
with the ease of music
they chew the heads off fish

when they are done they are almost out to sea
but with the practised nonchalance of Spring rain
they are beneath the surface
& swim up the river again
my love, are we like the otters

do we drift
& do we swim back?

IN THURSO ONE NIGHT

They slip under the eiderdowns of their bodies
the young boys in the bar
resisting their fears & talking about Rangers

how they could be blessed by the soft salt dew
I feel in my hair
this morning as I walked out

to the Firth, 'Be strong & then be gentle'
I wanted to cry out to them
'Like those warriors when your country

was young, men who drew their women
to them as lovingly as sheaves of corn
& only put steel through hatred

don't waste your hearts on the tired
organisations of boredom'
That I didn't is part of my general failure

then the night shut like a windblown door
& Thurso seemed
to slide beneath the waves

a Caithness Atlantis
where love comes
from stones

Roddy Hamilton

SOLOMON GRUNDY

'Solomon Grundy, born on a Monday,' I think, as I wheel the wayward trolley through the chrome entrance barrier. 'Born on a Monday and... died on a Sunday.' For the life of me I can't think what the fuck he did in between times and, even more absurdly, the more I try to think about it the more names of the seven dwarfs come to me, which is extremely infuriating considering that that was *last* week's quiz. The week before that had been 'name the seven deadly sins'. I got avarice and sloth (sloth I remembered because of the two-toed sloth of South America), and then I wondered if greed was also one. But then, avarice *is* greed, isn't it?

Droopy... Sneezy... Bashful... Apples need *apples*, not that I eat apples ever, at any time, but they look good on the table in the rest-room, in that nice Caithness glass bowl I got from Auntie Dotty. Poor Auntie Dotty, she's got dermatitis – her fingers are like beech twigs, My uncle says that'll teach her to go pulling on things she shouldn't, but I've not to say he says that.

Not very busy tonight, I think. Great thing this late night shopping. Wander around in a kind of shopping trance, picking up biscuits and looking at women. Perhaps it should be the other way around, I think, putting down a packet of Burton's Fig Rolls. The label reads, 'THAT GREAT DATE TASTE AND NO SHITTING'.

Eating things in supermarkets is very rude so usually I restrain myself and shoplifting is out. Nowadays with closed circuit televisions, mirrors like inverted satellite dishes in every corner...

It just isn't worth it, I think, and I shove a small bunch of bananas down my trousers.

I go to the potato stall, a little further along. The bananas bounce reassuringly in my pants like cold fruity fingers and I smile at the sensation. A small, brittle-looking woman who I'm sure did not see me casts me a disappointed glance then hobbles away towards onions.

There are Egyptian potatoes and Cypriot potatoes, and these are smoother, balder potatoes with less muck on them. I think it's because they have come such a long way. The Scottish potatoes are much grubbier. In fact as I peer into the crate it appears to be only earth and rocks. Before I can stop it my arm is in there, scrabbling and scraping like the unruly tentacle of an excited octopus and a gritty fog is rising from the box making me cough and splutter. My face emerges, slightly oranged by the soil particles, I see from the security mirror; and the small brittle lady who I decide looks like Thora Hird is staring again.

I stare back.

After choosing my bag from the dispenser by the scales, I decide on Kerrs pinks. These are particularly suited to mashing. I make a mental note to get butter when I reach *Dairy Products*.

Quiet though it is, there is an unusually high proportion of small boys and girls running around and this irks me somewhat. There is a proper place in which one should exercise young children. Playparks and such like are designated for their use and to bring them into this busy environment which is both dangerous and non-educational...

'*Little boy!*' I say.

His cuff is a long way down, I have to stretch. I bend further. Eye to eye.

'Stop running about and shouting or the boy-eating dragon will eat you, yum, yum, yum.'

I lick my lips and straighten up. The kid looks amazed but his brown rabbity eyes sense the danger. He scuttles off in search of his mum, one cuff of his parka nearly touching the floor, flapping like a prosthetic.

I have enough vegetables now. *Eat your greens! Eat your greens!* That's what Mummy said. And, of course, she was right. Most root vegetables – like parsnips, beetroots, carrots and the like – are high in vitamin B; and the other ones like onions and leeks are choc-full of vitamins C and A.

Fruits are also very good for this. A single orange contains the daily vitamin C requirement of a healthy adult. Uh-oh, the child's mother is coming over here.

It takes too long to hide behind the bread counter, although I try, but the four bags of potatoes make my trolley sluggish and a lawless front wheel leaves me stranded. She screeches something at me but I can't hear -- I'm too embarrassed. Then she looks as if she'll hit me but whirls away. The boy looks back. I cross my eyes and scrunch up my nose. I'm embarrassed for her. A little later, when everyone who was staring at her carries on their business, I take out the bananas because they're hurting my legs.

I have seven pills to take in the morning; three before breakfast and four after breakfast. I usually have Weetabix but today they only had Rice Krispies. I always find it amazing that the actual mass of a crushed dry Rice Krispie is only about five per cent of the original mass, but a Rice Krispie soaked in milk when pressed onto a table or plate will remain almost the same. Weetabix always expands in milk but the mass of a dry Weetabix when crushed is generally constant.

I decide to return with the bananas. They have become softer and the stalk has snapped slightly so I put them back and head for the freezer counter.

I like to stick my head in the freezer counter for as long as I can. It is a weird sensation. While down there I remember the four remaining dwarfs – Sleepy, Doc, Sneezy and Ugly. I wonder what a frozen fish finger would taste like. I look around but they aren't watching and so I gingerly peel the cardboard corner of a packet and take one out. I break it in two and place one bit in my mouth. Ooh, cold.

An assistant passes by with a mountain of sugar bags on a trolley. I smile breadcrumbs at him then quickly close my mouth. There's nowhere to put the fish finger because he is watching me. It is too big to swallow, so I chew it but it is too hard. Quickly, I lean into my trolley, under the auspices of re-arranging my four bags of potatoes, and the fish finger falls from my mouth to the floor, rattling through the bottom bars of my trolley. A glistening stream of saliva follows it but I unhook this with my forefinger and shake it off. The assistant doesn't seem to notice; he is shaking his head and walking away, his giant block of sugar bags rumbling down the aisle.

Feeling guilty, I take the opened box of fish fingers and take another six boxes as well. When I get home I will cook them. Must get spaghetti shapes, I think. I make a mental note.

I do a very smelly fart around the ready-meals area. It hovers odiously above the freezer before falling in.

With a pang of embarrassment I move away but before turning the corner into 'Soups and Beverages', watch as the pensioner who looks like Thora Hird pops the frozen fart into her basket.

At the delicatessen counter, you take a ticket from a roll. The ticket has a number on it and you wait for your number to be called. I know this because only last week I took a ticket from the used basket and waited for one hour and ten minutes. This week I leave the delicatessen counter alone. The salami sausages I eventually got did not appear to mix with my medication last week and having eaten them in the store found I was caught short on the bus journey home. Luckily I was at the back of the bus and nobody saw me shit myself.

So I skip the delicatessen counter and go and look at the fish counter. The little boy is there in the queue. His mother is talking to somebody else's mother. But no-one is behind the counter so I sneak round by the side to get a better look. I want to see them close, how their scales reflect whole rainbows of colours, how their eyes are so slimy; and now I am right up close. I eat a bit of parsley then spit it out. It is plastic. Then I reach out and pluck out the eye of a big fish.

The small boy winces. His mouth is open, his eyebrows point up in the middle. He tugs at mummy but I am round in an instant – as if I'd never even been behind the counter. The boy begins to cry as he pulls at mummy's coat. I panic as the two women suddenly turn round. I crash into my trolley and it pirouettes like an ice skater. I put the eye in my mouth. It is sticky, I don't want to swallow it. I feel sick.

She's coming over to me, the mother. Her face very angry. She's walking fast and I'm walking away – backwards – shaking my head, crying a little bit and trying desperately not to swallow the salty blob in my mouth. She screams 'YOU!', meaning me, and I turn, crashing right into a display of Roses chocolates. In the distance I seem to hear a voice say, *'Say thank you with a box of Cadbury's Roses'* and then my guts wrench and a torrent of yellow liquid erupts from my throat all over my trousers ('Oh no, not another pair!' I hear myself think), all over the scattered boxes of chocolates, all over the shiny marble floor, and I see the woman with her hands flat against her open mouth, aghast and distraught. Two assistants in white coats run over (oh, no, this is *all* too familiar). My trolley is still rolling around in circles. I feel drowsy again. There are a lot of people watching. *'Solomon Grundy,'* I think, *'Born on a Monday.'* Fuck this is terrible. *'Died on a Sunday.'*

'You OK son?' he says. He's got a grey beard. He doesn't look angry.

'Dies on a Sunday,' I think. I look at him feverishly and all around at the crowd that is gradually forming. *'Solomon Grundy,'* I think, and the fish-eye on my knee winks.

Brian Johnstone

THE WORKING CLASS CUP

This is the working class cup. You take it
from the cupboard where it rests, a lonely
isolate upon the shelf, its only
neighbours anything you can not quite fit
in space elsewhere. I stand and stare. Can it
be true that you have kept this cup solely
for tradesmen, as you say? I cruelly
taunt you with accusatory remarks but
can not dissuade you, cannot turn my wit,
show you this absurdity's completely
out of date. I hide the cup discreetly
in a box, in hopes that you'll forget it
in the move. Some chance. It knows its place.
Next visit, on the bottom shelf, replaced.

David Kinloch

JACOB AND THE ANGEL

Ay. Pause. Ah said pause. Och fuck it! Ye're past it. Past it!
Rewind!What? Ay. Jist tryin. Tryin tae get the shot. In focus
like. Difficult what with the grainy downslide. But ye've goat
tae try. Hit the button. Jeezus! Naw! It wizny him. But
somewun, some*thin*. Look ye can see him. Through the spray.
Just. Yon adam's apple. The hollow at the base. Bone
coloured skin. Ay aw skin an bone he wiz. Feathery hair.
Ah'm the cropped wan. Och fur speed, jimmy! Fur speed!
Whit d'*you* think! Hit the button fur chrissake. He pushed
ma button ah kin tell ye! Pain. Ecstasy. Aw wun in'it? *We*
know that! Ay. That's it! Tha's it! Is that a... Christ! It's a
fuckin claw! Ah've been tangoin wi a bear! Naw, mair like a
cat! What a bitch! Scream or cum? Below the belt anyway.
Below the fuckin belt. God ah wiz goodlookin in them days.
Even wi ma gob open! Squirmin. He knew it, jealous bastard.
Och look at the slaw-motion tear. Hold yer finger oan it.
Constant-like. Ay well. Ah'm jist numb now. It's all over. Has
been fur years. Now and again ah rewind. Try tae catch that
moment when ah wiz forced tae change, get a life. When ah
woke up in hospital they undid the straps and ah coudny
remember a thing. No even ma name. But the pain, the fuckin
pain! An ache in ma crotch the size ae a country.

THE HUNT

One sleepless night,
Stargazing by the flagpole in Queen's Park,
Thugs tried to shaft my neighbour
With his telescope
Sure he was a 'poof'.

He joked himself away,
Regaled us at a Close meeting
With his close shave,
While I silently recalled
An unforgettable park dusk:
The sound of padding sneakers
On the paths, the reek of over-
Ripe laburnum, poppers in a copse

And the sudden, shaking gallop
Of a mounted cop all caped and
Kaisered, lightbrigading our intense
Brief scatter at an incline
Through the grass, the shrieking

Neigh, the curse and crash,
Then, through the deep blue
Twilight, the wracking sobs
As a figure bent across his ruined
Horse: at my quiet feet
The splayed and helpless animals.

Norman Kreitman

WANTED

I need a cheerful dwarf to bring me silver
in solids slabs of filigree to meet my many needs.

Then friends arriving by steamer at the pier
could see my rings flash 'Welcome' in morse-code.

Money would be easy; he's send new-minted shillings
enthusiastic to leap into my hand.

My last table-fork could go walkabout
and he'd conjure up its twin, dutiful, sedate

or if a filling should drop out of my tooth
one pinch would settle that treachery.

And when the storm drives slates upon my head
I would wear a shining helmet, and be happy.

Sometimes he and I would sing together;
Edwardian duets, wistful and tender.

Best of all, I'd hold him tightly by the hand
when returning through the suburbs late at night
and the lights go out, one by one.

THE EXTRA

'I'll say this only once,' said the director,
massaging his temples.
'You're gangsters, see, very tough, sitting around
drinking in this bar.
Charlie here runs in with a warning.
You all leap up
and run out after him. Two takes only,
and no cock-ups.
After that you get your money.'

Later, idling towards my room,
panning past billboards
losing their skins, drifting through the longshot
of the market at night
as a different life emerged from the shadows,
I appreciated the warmth
in my wallet, and felt grateful to that man
who explained things
so clearly, that for two whole minutes
I understood the plot.

Alex Laird

WRITERS GROUP

Hiv a swatch it this batch:
He flicked a wheen sheets o paper
Doon on the table top.
Pretendin tae be cool an wazie
Aboot the hale thing.

Ahch, a jist gethert thum the gither,
Cleanin oot the drawers ye micht say.
Leanin back in his chair
He flicked a fag fae its packit.
Ahh, bit whin he wis lichtin it
The tremmil in his haun
Telt me the truth o it.

Richt awa a kent he hud sweatit
In the early hours, takin oot an pittin in
Mooned aboot fur days afore gein it birth.
Jist like the rest o us.

Wrasult wi the inklin tae tell it as it wis,
Wrasult wi the tear
Held it in the ee till it swalt fu
An gie near drookin the paper it fell on.

Maurice Lindsay

NEWARK PRIORY

Each year I pass, blown centuries of weather
have thinned more from these walls. Roofed better days,
sheltered austerity; the trembling feather
of breathing channelled into droning praise:

praise for a gift prayed back to whence it came
by those afraid to use it; whose retreat
made flickering candles greater than the game
monks shuffled over stones on sandalled feet.

Cementing faith that purposed certainty
has cracked and split, its man-made dogmas felled;
like grandeured stones without a holding key
to glory what false legend once compelled.

For years now, motorists have scarcely glanced
at ruined dominance left out to grass,
belief's self-rapt hysteria untranced,
the wrenching munch of cows its only Mass.

Gerry Loose

hurrying lines

on my cycle looking for buddhas & wild flowers   back on
the island in mind   it's the one thing

met Paul practising his penny whistle in deserted North
Woodside Road on his way to an AA meeting

Stan tells me Gerard Manley Hopkins stayed in N Woodside
Road six weeks

while Biddy thirteen again June again sings herself into sleep
meeting herself again sister again grandmother again my
heart again this

way is clear I hurry to meet John it's the one thing on the
arched footbridge that's over the road over the motorway
tunnel where

a man carries another who is upright facing over the carrier's
shoulder and puts him down near the end of the footbridge

he then walks backwards in the direction he has come while
the carried man remains unmoving

until the carrying man reaches the point of the arc where he
is disappearing from the carried man's view

who then jumps on the spot arms at his side everyone I carry
pauses at the corner to watch

with my rucksack heavy with his books I hurry to meet John
at noon at the Tron but first everything carried watches 5
young men

watch a 6th make photocopies from John's book and arrived
ordering tea wait for John

Nicol Mackintosh

GETTING STARTED

Buzz... buzz... buzz. Sweep left hand sideways. Alarm clock bounces off wall. Buzzing stops. Open eyes. Clock reads seven-thirty. Close eyes just for a moment. Open then. Digits now eight-forty-seven. Magic – time travel. Blink once to see what happens. Still eight-forty-seven.

'Mark! Mark! Are you ready yet?' Mum's voice comes scraping up the stairs. Leap out of bed, catch toe in sheet, tumble over, collide with wardrobe, land on carpet, pain seeping into knee and shoulder. Hobble to bathroom. Mum's assault continues. 'The interview's at nine-thirty, for goodness' sake.'

Got the wrong shirt. Drag it off, rummage, fumble, on with new one. These the right underpants? Probably doesn't matter. No time for getting knocked down by a car.

'Mark, come on!' Six weeks since I left school, and she's been on at me to get a job every day, double time at weekends. Does she know about the three million unemployed? Rush downstairs. Pour out cornflakes, grab carton of milk from fridge, tear at the top, squirt milk over my jacket. Mum wipes me down, muttering pagan curses.

'Forget breakfast, just get going.' She scowls at my hair, straightens my tie, stuffs a clean handkerchief into my pocket. 'Don't show yourself up. You don't know when you'll get another chance.'

'OK, OK.' Can't think of more detailed reassurance.

Escape outside and race to bus stop. Rain starting. No time to run back for umbrella. Bus appears just as water seeping into left shoe. Time now nine fifteen. Shuffle forward.

'How much to the Mountcross Industrial Estate?'

'One pound ten.'

Aah! No change.

'Get a bloody move on, son.' Driver sounds just like Mum. Perhaps a bit more affectionate. 'Look, are you getting on or not?'

Shove two pounds into machine, take ticket, stumble to seat. They said I could claim travel expenses. Is that the official fare, or what I really spent? I could be down by ninety pence already. Financial ponderings interrupted by gurgling sound. Small child is leaning over from seat in front. Smile back weakly. It drools expertly and slimily over right leg of my trousers. Frantically search in pockets for a tissue. Find just the handkerchief inserted by maternal instinct. Consider the possible downside of having to blow my nose on a drool-enriched hankie. A glutinous glob is establishing itself on my right knee. Poke feebly at it. End up spreading the stain. Suppose trousers now match my semi-skimmed jacket. Try to forget this and think positive thoughts. What did they tell us at school about interviews? Not much, far as I remember.

Bus screeches and rattles to a halt. We're past my stop. Leap up, rush to door, jump off, sleeve catches on handle, jacket lining tears, slip on wet pavement, land on my back. In a puddle. Rain even heavier now. Ten minutes late already. Sprint back several hundred yards. Other shoe now surrendering to the damp. Face red, no breath left.

The building squats among grimy portakabins. Reception area is warm and bright. Receptionist isn't. Sit down sweatily on a plastic chair and see if I have any thoughts to gather. Try to ignore drips from my clothes. Inspect the floor intently. Mottled beige, like school steamed pudding. Cracks everywhere. And two black shiny shoes. Female shoes. Nylon-clad feet in them. Brain still on defrost, my eyes pan upwards. Slim ankles, nice calves, knees OK, thighs... waaow. A trim grey skirt, black belt, well filled white blouse, grey jacket. Silky, wavy hair round a really cute face. Oh shit, she's watching me. Watching her. Blush rapidly and thoroughly. Hang on, she doesn't seem embarrassed, offended, outraged, vengeful. She smiles. 'Hi.'

I stare back. C'mon, try a smile. The one you use on dribbling infants. 'Hi.'

'Mark, isn't it?'

Desperately try to engage brain. 'Uhuh. Yeah. Mark.' She does look a bit familiar. Don't know any smart birds like this, though.

'You're Brian's pal. I'm Chrissie.' Chrissie. Chrissie? Do I know a Chrissie? 'Mind, I was in 4B when you were in 4D. Chrissie Duncan.'

Jeez. Christine Duncan. Scruffy wee brat with spots, specs, and straggly hair. She's transformed herself into this? Discover my mouth is hanging open.

'Oh aye. Chrissie. Right.'

'You here for the interviews?'

'Yeah, the interviews.'

This repartee must please her. She smiles again. 'They've done me already. They asked me to wait.'

'Oh.'

Receptionist interrupts my torrent of wit, herds me into an inner office. Three men in suits behind a big table. All carefully ignoring me. Try to tuck the lining back into my sleeve. Sit down. Big bald guy in the middle raises his eyebrows just a bit.

'Do sit down, Mr... Ellis.'

'Oh. Right.'

'Would you like a cup of coffee?'

'Uh... yeah, thanks.'

Receptionist frowns at me. Or could be her idea of a smile. 'Milk and sugar?'

'Yeah, please.'

Can't stand white sugary coffee, but accepting seems the line of least resistance. She exits, lips clamped together. Bald guy turns over some papers.

'Now, Mr Ellis, I see you left school this summer.'

'Yeah, that's right.'

'And you have passes in English and... ah... History?'

'Yeah, that's right.'

Receptionist returns. That was quick. Must be one of these vending machines with six variations on lukewarm brown liquid. I balance the polystyrene cup on the arm of my chair.

'And you've had no paid employment previously?' Thin grey bloke on the left now.

'Yeah, that's right.'

Maybe I could just have done this interview by postcard – one answer fits all.

'Could you tell us why you applied for this particular job?'

The round red face on the right this time. Swivel to face him, triggering the completely inevitable and totally predictable. Coffee cup topples over into my lap. Rise abruptly, projecting rest of coffee on to carpet.

'Aw hey, I'm sorry.'

They all seem to be holding their breath. Dab pathetically at trousers with handkerchief. Slight feeling of deja vu. Regret opting for milk and sugar. At least it camouflages the contribution from the gobbing infant.

Rest of interview flashes past. Must have lasted all of three minutes. Out to the waiting room again. Chrissie smiles. Does nothing erode her cheerfulness?

'How'd you get on?'

'Ah... not bad. S'pose.'

Receptionist waves a form at me. 'Mr Ellis, could you let me have your expense claim. Now. And Miss Duncan, could you go back in for a minute, please?'

Inspect the form. Lots of squares labelled 'For Official Use Only'. Someone once told me something witty to write in these boxes, but can't remember it now. OK, two pounds spent so far. What about the return trip? Another two pounds? I've even less change now – have to use a fiver. Maybe claim a fiver each way for consistency? Ten pounds? They'll get the Not Tremendously Serious Fraud Office on to me. Panic, and scribble something illegible.

Chrissie emerges, her smile wider, deeper, warmer and generally more gigantic than before. Her eyes, too.

'I got the job. Mark, I got it!'

'Oh. Congratulations. Yeah, great. Good.' Well, never really expected to get it. Seem to remember Christine – Chrissie – wasn't bad at passing exams, as well.

We step outside. No rain, no clouds, sun shining, streets gleaming.

'Are you heading back now?' Chrissie is pretty dazzling, too.

'Yeah. You too?'

She's standing close. 'Yes. Let's walk. It's beautiful now.'

We stroll back into town, chatting. She's great fun. Good sense of humour. We talk about folk we know, movies we like, other really deep issues. We get to the end of her street. She turns to face me.

'How about helping me celebrate tonight?'

'Celebrate? Oh, the job. Right. What do you fancy?'

'We could try that new place on Well Street. They sometimes have live music.'

'Great. Come round for you at seven?'

'OK. See you then.'

One last de luxe smile, a touch on my arm – a touch on my arm! – then she goes. I watch her as long as I can, then head home.

Mum ambushes me in the hall, frown screwed firmly in place. She looks at me. My clothes are soaked with a variety of fluids. My feet squelch. The lining is hanging out of my sleeve.

'So? How did you get on?'

I give a big smile. 'Marvellous. Just... marvellous.'

John Maley

BRIDGING THE ATLANTIC

Tony sat at the bar and watched Joanie wiggle his arse, pour endless pints and blink his big false eyelashes. Joanie had fallen in love. 'He's a Yank,' Joanie had beamed at Tony. 'Six feet two, eyes of blue. He's a computer software man. I'm only interested in his hardware.' Tony sipped his pint and nodded approvingly. He only sipped his pint because he had been so drunk the night before. It was nice to watch Joanie now. Suddenly transformed by love. Well, it that's what he wanted to call it who the fuck was Tony or anybody else to disagree?

Tony had tasted love. American style, too. He'd been to Bennets one night when he was cruised by a big beefy guy called Johnny. Think William Shatner and half the size again. He was a trolley dolly doing Boston–Glasgow runs. It was one of those ten to three nights. Ten to three and no man. Then of course the dance of the desperadoes started... Johnny appeared out of nowhere. At three o'clock they were in a taxi, heading for the Moat House hotel, Johnny's big right hand down the front of Tony's trousers. Sometimes you gave a fuck what the taxi driver thought and sometimes you didn't.

The hotel foyer seemed floodlit. Tony suddenly felt shy as he followed Johnny like a lost puppy dog through the foyer, past the bar area and into the lift. It being late it was just the two of them. Johnny turned to look at Tony with adoring eyes.

'You're so handsome.'

Tony liked the complimentary approach. He glanced up and down the length of Johnny's body and felt pleased with himself.

In the hotel room they took off their shoes, had a dry hump on the bed, then raided the mini-bar. Tony drank some gin and tonic as there was no beer. As he mulled over his drink he looked at Johnny stretched out on the bed. His tee-shirt had rode up revealing a big hairy belly. Two things came to Tony then. First, so much for trolley dollies being skinny male models. Second, there was no rapport. They had nothing to communicate to each other.

'Jerk me off.'

Tony sat astride Johnny and wanked him. Johnny closed his eyes and smiled contentedly. He might as well have been doing it himself. After he'd came Johnny wiped his belly with some tissues and pulled at Tony's zip.

'I'd like to return the compliment.'

During the night Tony woke and lay beside Johnny in the darkness. He listened to Johnny's breathing. He couldn't see his face. He could see the back of his head, his fine sandy brown hair, his broad bare back. Tony leaned forward to brush his lips tenderly against Johnny's back.

Walter Weinstein was the other American. He was older. Forty, maybe. Tony had been aware of Walter for some time. Walter's face had cropped up the whole night. Firstly, in Delilah's, through the smoke and the stench, he'd seen him smile. Then in Club X, Walter loitered in the shadows, smiling again. Smiling at Tony.

He had his own company. It was some kind of travel company. He gave Tony his card. It had on it the name of the company and 'Walter Weinstein, Company Director'. The sceptic in Tony thought anybody could have a card made up. 'Tony McCormack, President of the World'. But he had no reason not to believe Walter. They got a taxi to the Marriot. Tony would have walked.

Walter sat on the edge of the bed drinking a soda and lime. He wanted to talk. He talked about how beautiful Scotland was. How he travelled for business and pleasure. He talked about Ohio, where he lived and worked. Walter lived alone. He used to live with a guy as house buddies but got pissed with it. Walter said it's hard to live with another adult you're not having sex with. Tony felt so tired he lay down on top of the bed. It was then Walter began to take off his clothes, slowly and unself-consciously. Tony yanked at his own clothes. This wasn't going to be a shagging party. The tone of the evening had been set.

Once they were both under the covers, Walter turned off the bedside lamp. Everything seemed magnified, the sound of Walter swallowing, the creaks of the bed, the smell of Walter's aftershave, whatever it was. Walter put his arms around Tony. He held him so tight. Tony thought his ribs would crack. He was still in Walter's arms. This was all that was needed, this closeness.

In the morning the sun shone into the room. Walter made small talk and coffee and they sat on the unmade bed. Walter looked older and sadder in the morning. Tony was usually depressed after a one-night stand. It used to be guilt a long time ago but now it was just the alcohol and wondering how the fuck to get home. Then again, Walter had further to go home than he did. After a while they fell quiet. Tony thought about hotel rooms and how they seemed to have been especially designed for casual sex. He thought it was a good idea. Neutral territory. Neither was at home here.

They each had a shower. Tony smelled the stale cigarette smoke that had stuck to the Brylcreem on his hair. His eyes were bloodshot and his hair was defying gravity. As he dried himself he thought he could hear Walter whistle in the room.

Showered and dressed, Walter and Tony stood a foot apart at the window. Walter had opened the curtains and they both looked out at the city below. They never said a word. They just stood there, looking out at the city, bathed in strong winter sunlight. It was as if they were both trying to remember who they were, where they were.

John Manson

[LUVE RAIS BITWEEN WIZ]

Luve rais bitween wiz,
lek the mune bitween twa palm trees
that hae niver touchit.

Luve innard trummill o twa bodies
swalled til a lullaby,
bit the roupit throt wis rittit.
The lips wir stanes.

The langour til haud steered the flesh,
it lichted up the kennilled banes,
bit whan the airms ettilled til streitch out
they crumpilled as they met.

Luve passit lek a mune bitween wiz
and et up wir lanely bodies.
And we're twa ghaists wha luik fur ane anither
and meet a lang wey awa.

'Luve rais bitween wiz' is a translation of
'El amor ascendía entre nosotros', which was
untitled, by Miguel Hernández (1910–1942).

Brian McCabe

from *Low Life*

BUZZARD

I'm a big bad bastard.
I've done too much solitary.
Watch this. I'll empty this tree
just by clearing my throat.
If anything runs or crawls
I'll claim it in my claw.
I'll tell you something else:
My ancestors were hawks
and vultures. I'm a serial killer.
But nowadays I've got you
to do the business for me.
In your flash steel feathers –
you're fast, I'll say that for you.
You'd make a good buzzard.
Seriously: you could be me.
I enjoy an uncooked breakfast.
Raw liver. Fresh intestines.
Especially when it's killed for me.

EEL

Listen to me brothers and sisters
we have come so far together
to reach the mouth of this river.
Now it's time to turn silver and black.
You can probably feel the salt water
changing the function of your kidneys.
This is normal. If we stay together
now, we can describe a wide arc
between Bermuda and Puerto Rico
till we come to our birthplace –
where the currents are sluggish
and the seaweed is dense –
the perfect spot to mate, spawn
and die. First we have to get there.

This sea is deep and dangerous.
Don't trust anybody – even your own
swallower and gulper cousins.
When those guys need to eat
all they do is open their mouths
and swim. This advice comes
from our ancestral memory:
trust in your sense of smell,
stay elusive and keep in line.
Okay on with the migration.
If anybody asks who we are
tell them we're snakes that swim
and we take forever to kill.

Let's go to the Sargasso.

COCKROACH

So look at it this way.
We share the same building.
So you let us know you're coming.
We make ourselves scarce.

We don't care if it's an apartment
overlooking Central Park
or an apartment overlooked
by the census.

We care about your garbage.
True the rich have more
than the poor – but they keep it
locked up, like their art.

We have our own culture.
In one of our modern fables
a cockroach wakes up to find
he has changed into a *man*.

We're out of here. We scatter
like the coffee beans you drop
when you see us, but faster.
So we disgust you. Suits us.

We can live on your disgust.
We are spreading north.
Soon we hope to inherit
whatever is left of the earth.

MUSSEL

Hello God, this is me
in my long blue burberry
with the shiny lining
sitting on my dorsal hinge
with my wee black bible
clasped tight in my shell
praying I'll no be noticed
by anybody bigger than me.
It would be good to travel
in the ballast water
of a transatlantic liner.
And to develop stripes.
A cousin of mine did that.
In the meanwhile I'll cling
to this rock of ages – or is it
just ages of rock? – anyway
please God, if you're there
– and I mean, even if you're not –
give me a grain of sand
and I'll turn it into a pearl.
At least let me procreate.

Mytilus, modiolus, mytildae.
Anodanta, unio, unionidae.

Amen.

Murdo MacLeod MacDonald
(Mac Mhurchaidh a Stal)

DIÙLTADH

Thuit mo dhàin leis a' chreig
Man bò m' athar
A chaill a beatha
'S an laogh a bha na broinn.
Ach thàinig mo laoigh fhìn
Air ais thugam sa phost
Càil ach beò,
An dèidh sgrùdadh mhuinntir
Dhùn Eideann
Nach do thuig gu robh
fìon nuadh sna searragan;
'Dè na searragan?' ars' iadsan,
'Na searragan a dh' fheumar
cruthachadh bho chraicinn mo laoigh!'

REFUSAL

My poems fell seabound
Like dad's cow
That got snuffed
With calf still in utero.
But my own babies
Came home
Barely breathing,
After an Edinburgh pounding
That didn't perceive
The newly bottled vintage;
'What bottles?' they ask,
'The ones which must be blown
From my own calfskins!'

AN DÀIMH NACH URRAINN A BHITH

Mhosgail a' mhadainn à suain na h-oidhche
Le fiaclan grèine a' cliobadh bheanntan Chataibh
Is Suilbhean na shuidhe air bathais na h-Alba
A' gabhail na grèine mar bu dual
'S ag amharc air Mùirneag –
Cagaran gaolach;
Ri sainnsearachd mar osagan Foghair
A-null thar sgìths na mara,
Gun euradh teanga;
Is canach an adhair
Na leabaidh bhuan
Ri dol a dhith
Air sgàthan a' Chuain Sgìth.

UNREQUITED LOVE

The morning woke from nightsleep;
Sun-rays nibbling Sutherland's peaks;
Suilbhean resting on Scotland's brow,
Taking the sun like a legacy
And looking across to Mùirneag –
Little darling;
Whispering like tireless Autumn eddies
Across a jaded sea;
The bog-cotton sky –
An empty bed
Gone to waste
In the mirror of The Minch.

BÀRDACHD

Streath dhubhan' ann an siopaigeadh
Mo smuaintean;
Is m' fhacail –
Peile loma-làn de bhiathadh;
Lugaichean 'son a' chreagaich.
Ach de 'm feum a th' anns an driomlach
Mana bi gad dhàn
Air bàrr mo shlait
Aig deireadh an latha?!

POETRY

My thoughts –
A line of prepared hooks;
My words –
A pail full of bait;
Lugworms for the rock-fishing.
But, at the end of the day,
What use is the tackle
If there isn't a bundle of poems
Hanging from my rod?!

GAOL MARA

Dha-na-trì uairean san latha
Dh'fhairich mi blas
Do phògan saillt'
A' bristeadh a-steach orm
Mar bu dual,
'S a' struthadh bhuam
Mar a bhiodh dùil,
'S tu muigh an siud
Nad choileach geal
Ach seo thu rithist
Nad chabhaig bhlàith,
Le neart do ghaoil
A' slìobadh mo bhroillich
'S a' diogladh mo shliasaid
'S a' laighe orm dreiseag –
Maise do lànachd
Nach seasadh pluc –
Ach tràghadh dhìom
Gu bràth.

SEA LOVE

Two or three times a day
You showered me
With a salt kiss
Inheritance
Slipping from me
As expected,
And you out there
In billowing whiteness
Coming again
In warm speed
Love's might
Caressing my body
Tickling my thigh
And lying on me
A while –
The ephemeral beauty
Of your eagerness
Ebbing
From me forever.

Carl MacDougall

THE FORTUNE TELLER

He shivered and thought he was sickening for something, every now and then looking up from his desk when she crossed his mind like smoke.

For she'd come up from nowhere, just arrive; sometimes it was everything, the look, feel, smell, taste and touch of her; or it began with an image, something fresh, the way her teeth overlapped, light trapped in her hair, the shape of her neck or the tattoo on her arm; a swallow with the tail pointing at her shoulder, a red and blue swallow with a yellow shadow, three red hearts entwined and GEO along the bottom.

I thought I was in love, she said. Well, I was in love, but not any more.

I think they're ugly.

My mother had a butterfly. For six years she said it was a transfer and I believed her. I thought she washed it every night and put it back in the morning. I think I'll get that done, a butterfly. My father's got the Face of Christ across his chest and an eagle down his back. Then he's got my mother's name, my name, my sister's name, my brother's name, Mum and Dad and Scotland on his arms. He's got a kiltie dancer on this arm and a sword up here.

You're fine as you are.

Everybody says that, but I'd like to lose a few pounds, I would like to lose some weight, just to know there were clothes I could wear.

She was beautiful and supple with eyes the colour of amber, soft skin, carmine hair and the vintage radiance of a Raeburn painting. She dressed with tenuous ease, tan leather shoes, oatmeal trousers, green silk blouse and a gold necklace with amber in the crown of a filigreed decoration. When he saw her, he stared, as though she was an illusion, a school friend who'd been raised from the dead.

Someone told him, Go and see her.

He'd thought about it, not really knowing what to expect. Then pavements overwhelmed him. The rush and expectancy, the carelessness of others was disconcerting. On the way home from work, he suddenly dreaded being alone and stood still as a lamp or a telephone kiosk. Then he turned and walked the three miles to her door, standing outside to make sure he was right, watching the men who looked either way as the entry closed behind them.

She read neither palms nor heads, did not examine eyes or charts, consult the moon, read eggs in water, tea leaves, fire or crystal balls, confer tarot or playing cards, astrological charts, discuss phases of the suns and planets. She read men.

I see red eyes coughing, she said. I see money and you must be careful of a dark-haired woman who's younger than you. I think you've met her, but can't be sure. Your work is very demanding and you are keen to get promotion. Is there a Colin or a Calum in your work? He'll get the promotion. I see life and growth and nothing else, excepting love: you'll fall in love.

How do you know?

It speaks to me.

What does it say?

Nothing just now. It's nearly asleep. And he's not like you, he doesn't talk in his sleep. Come back when he's wakened, when he's ready to talk, when there's something to say.

Two nights and a day: he neither shaved nor changed his clothes and scarcely washed. He shook his head when the girls in the office asked how he was; the boss had said he ought to go home, so he left his desk and walked out the building.

He thought he heard someone singing as he roamed the streets teeming with tourists. Sometimes another voice mingled with the song of a busker, but it seemed to be like a country pub he'd often imagined, the sort of place where they brewed their own beer, where fiddlers played and singing started at the back of nine, a place without entertainment, where ghosts were laid and dreams revived.

Towards evening he wandered through the park where women swung their sons in the air and the men played football, where low shouts drifted through the skies like swifts. Women gathered their children and lead them to the gate while the men played on. He watched the earnest reading, students going home, the couples on the grass. He saw the old women feeding ducks dipping their hands in a brown paper bag, tearing the bread with a sudden ferocity, waiting till the ducks had eaten, till they scurried round each other and ploughed the water with their beaks. And just as they were about to break, to search another part of the pond, the bread cartwheeled through the air, landing with a soft splash; ripples from successive pieces collided.

Evening light fingered the sky. He passed a pub door and a dog barked. Inside, the rush had just begun. Did you hear this? a fat man asked, as the barman poured two pints, looked up and glisked him standing by the door.

This guy meets his pal in a pub.

What's up? says the pal.

Bloody wife, the man says.

Is she still giving you bother?

Do dogs pish in the street.

I'll tell you what, the pal says. Ride her to death.

Will it work?

Never known to fail.

How long'll it take?

Three weeks.

So the guy's not seen in the pub for ten days, maybe a fortnight, and one night the pal's passing his close and thinks he'll look up to see how he is.

The wife comes to the door looking fifteen years younger, singing, hair permed, new dress, all made up, high-heeled shoes. Hello, she says. In you come. He is in bed.

The pal's propped up on four pillows. Fucked. Looks like death, lost weight, smoking like a tinker's fire, hands and lips trembling, just dovering, neither here nor there.

Here's your pal to see you, the wife says.

How's it going? says the pal.

Hard work.

Your wife's looking well but.

Aye. Poor bitch. She doesnae know she's only got a week to live.

By the gantry, the barman unfolded his arms. As he lifted the counter, the fat man shouted, Right lads. Free bar, his laughter rising above the noise.

Out, said the barman.

Her ghost mingled with a photograph he had seen in a men's magazine. Ten naked women calf deep in the sea, Danish women, certainly Scandinavian, no more than twenty one or two, narrow hips and blonde hair, staring at the camera, and at the centre, a Caribbean woman who walked in the shade.

He smiled as the barman grabbed an arm, swung him round and used his head to propel him through the door, bleeding on to the empty street. Now people stared as the city moved around him; and she was still, at the centre of the photograph, smiling.

His father smoked Capstan down to the quick. His sister became a dreary anorexic after their mother died clutching her Bible by the side of the road as the blue ambulance light paled the faces in the crowd. The last thing he'd heard her say was that she fancied going to the evening service; it was a while since she'd been.

Do what you like, his father had said.

The school inspectors called, then social workers. When his sister was taken to hospital, he found his father weeping by the fire. I've no cigarettes, he said.

With his sister in and out the place and everybody calling her daft, the last time he visited her, she said she was in love with one of the patients and was getting a job. She worked in a fast food place and came home with stories about what the men did to the food.

On his last night home, his father called his sister a hoor, still shouting when he went to bed, banging the furniture around in his room, yelling on his wife in heaven to look after their children.

He packed his rucksack and stood at the bus station. The first bus said Glasgow, so he got on board and ran around town in the rain till he found a room and got a job. After a month, the boss asked if he fancied college to learn the work.

God Almighty, someone said, a student, a girl who lived in the flat. God Almighty, look at your face. And you're filthy. Did somebody rob you?

He lay on the bed while she washed his face and put cream on his cuts. Help me in, he said. Put me to bed.

She told him how hard it was living on a grant, especially when the cheques were six weeks late. There's money in the drawer, he said. Take what you need.

Holy Mary Mother of God, she said. Where did you get this?

It's wages, he said. I worked for it.

Some of these packets aren't even opened. You want to put this money in the bank, someplace safe.

It's fine and handy where it is. I take what I need.

I'll pay you back, she said. I swear to God, I'll pay you back.

She took some notes and put out the light.

He wakened with her face before him, the image of her kneeling to read his fortune. He turned himself over, returned to sleep, then prised his eyes open. The eyelids were sticky. His mouth was bitter, he had a headache and his nose was blocked. He coughed to remove what he thought were secretions in his chest. Again, he slept and prised his eyes open. His body was sticky, his hands and fingers cold. He lay till evening when he slept again, his hands round his groin, imagining he was a plant in need of water.

When he wakened the room was filled with light. He trembled in the bathroom, threw water on his face and waited for the kettle to boil. With the kitchen full of steam, he made coffee, dense and black in a cup that barely held a mouthful. With every sip, he felt restored.

He came out the shower, his hair anointed with the scent of flowers. He unwrapped three presents he'd got last Christmas from the girls at work. The first was face balm, the last after shave. There was a multicoloured tie. He took a grey suit from the wardrobe, one of the two he'd never worn, and unpacked a new white shirt, being careful of the pins. When he was putting on his new striped socks, there was a tap at the door.

You all right? It was the skinny guy who never worked and lived across the hall.

Fine.

Is it an interview?

Uh-hu.

I heard you were ill.

I'm fine now.

Fancy a coffee?

Just had one.

Listen. He came into the room. I heard a great joke.

Lassie tells her Da she's pregnant.

Who did it?

Wee Sammy McAllister up the High Street.

So the father pulls on his jacket, goes up to the house and batters the door. There's a rattle of chains and bolts, takes ages to open and a wee guy's there with no arms.

You Sammy McAllister?

Aye.

Know Jeannie McCausland?

Aye.

Fine, says the father and away he goes, back to the house

where the lassie's at the sink washing the dishes.
The father gives her an almighty wallop.
Jesus Christ, she says. What have I done?
Wallop, goes the father.
What's that for? says the lassie.
That, says the father, is for helping yourself.
Very good.
I don't suppose you could help me out?
Sorry, pal. No can do.
Have you nothing at all?
Nothing spare. The lassie that said I was ill has money.
You've a cut on your forehead.
It's healing up.
Are they new shoes?
I'm sorry to be rude, but I have to go.
Aye, all right then, as long as you're fine.

He closed the door and fixed his black buckled shoes. He took his money from the drawer, opened the packets and divided the notes in denominations, put the change in the bag that had held the shoes, pulled the strings and for the first time he could remember locked the door of his room and left with the key in his pocket.

She smiled. Feeling better?
Fine, he said.
I want to tell your fortune. I can see your future. It is ready to be told. She took him upstairs, into her room.
I see money and love, fields and harvests, the colour blue and the number seven.

She asked him to tell of the women he'd known, held his head when he cried and they rocked back and forward: There, baby, there. There, there, there. It's all right now. There, baby, there.

It was easier to let him do what he wanted, she said, easier to say yes than cause any argument, easier to give in. Look what happened when I wanted more. Look what happened when I didn't give in.

And he held her to him. There, he said. there, there, there.

It was Isa the cleaner who saw them leave. She came in every morning, made tea for the folk still hanging around, polished the glass and dusted the tables, cleaned the carpets, emptied ashtrays and ordered taxis for those who wished to leave.

She said they came out the room together, she with an outdoor coat, suitcases and a small leather bag. He smiled and she said, Cheerio, Isa.

The last sound was the click of her heels on the stair.

James McGonigal

DRIVEN HOME

I am the angel charged to take you home.
I have nothing to look forward to. You have.

You think you nodded off for forty winks:
big boy, you have been dozing for a hundred years.

And here we are on Purgatory's M8
blinking awake by floodlit Kirk o' Shotts

where rusted tv masts and riding lights
pitch above Central Scotland's forest's waves.

Here's Holytown and Newhouse. Sing the one
about your father's many mansions. Hope it's true.

They're gathered at the door to see you in.
Loosen your seatbelt. There's our Maker – no,

that bloke with silver stubble on his chin
and five scenes from your famous childhood

tattooed on each forearm. On you go.

THE NITHSDALE SONNETS

1.

Gless, fu gless, an oorsels the amber in it,
bringin past tae future in yin gleg lift frae table
tae tongue. Bright blooddrops shook on clumps
of fuchsia fleering all summer at the Solway.
Cattle were driven to mart along sunk roadways
with never a cry, seldom a gull or an adder in sight,
even the dogs silent, heads down to nip at slow hooves;
nothing else here but two lumps of lads herding
Ayrshires whose udders squirt light.
And each day winked its hooded eye: changeable
whichever way you scanned it, grey or green showers,
shadows or a yellow fierce as your father's face.
Who shakes us awake, who's been out in the field
already ploughing for hours.

2.

We had come back to Gallowa, its kailyards long
smoothed out by rain and money. A robin pecked
among red-breasted leaves of strawberries
seeded on a grassy dyke; beyond, a ditch's song:
loose knots of foam unravelling in its throat.
There were two brothers executed by this road
to Moniaive. Muscles slipped like water at the sight
of them grown grey as out at dawn they strode
to meet their Christ. Who could sidestep the sound of shots
or feel their faith untainted by the stink? Speuggies alight
to peck at roadside grit. It seems our blood has split
asunder: like peaty pools of Scaur we used to
fling ourselves into as bairns – yin loup
wi shut een, riskin it.

3.

Seeking among Nith rocks to find, to reach
for and lose again: each day we strained
to copy down dictation from the measured speech
of trout pools. One of us almost mastering the art
of blackie sol-fa from the bankside sauchs (am I
saying that right?) forgot the luckless gasp as ice
unchained itself from roots, grey waters turning
over then like sleepers in one bed to dream apart.

We crossed by the forge and the old bridge reeled
as we trod the length of its arm outstretched
to the farther bank, one horny hand concealed
in its glove of grass. Then down night falls
and stars fly up to shine above, like sweat revealed
on blacksmiths' faces working their hot coals.

4.

Hae we nae bucht to shelter in? Gorse, thornwood,
everything tugged sideways by souwesterlies. A ram poised
there between his granite gates, guarding the brood:

those years all gathered into twists of wool
caught in a cleft. Older now, our merest smile is just
what the air says, opening its lips to breathe a full

day, indraw a cup of tears then out another dawn:
what it says is *wheesh, tilliewhillie* (that's a light at six)
and *och nae wonder your faither's gane*

(the wind under the door at seven). So we're taking
the langrig road home now as leaves go sprinting
before us and the wind carries stories away. Hinting

that what we never exactly wish for comes to pass,
unkempt ponies by the gate accept our fresh tugged grass.

Ciara MacLaverty

FRIED SCAMPI FROM HELL

Vicky visits me every Saturday lunch time at the shop cause she knows my boss always goes to the Harbour Inn for a plate of fried scampi.

'Frankenstein's gone then?' she asks but it is more of a statement than a question. It was Vicky who named him Frankenstein because of his silent hovering and his funny eye. Now as soon as the bell tinkles behind him I start to breathe easier. We sit with our bums on the radiator and keep an eye on the customers. Usually if I'm lucky they don't have to ask for my help and they know what size of jeans to buy. I let them take a bit pile into the changing room anyway. There's no curtain in the window cause it looks straight out over the sea. Me and Vicky laugh and imagine how stupid we would feel if we were starkers and a fishing boat could see right in.

'God, imagine if it was *his* boat,' she says, 'mortification or what?' I don't bother asking her the exact meaning of 'mortification' but I guess it roughly means she'd take a beamer.

Like she took a major beamer last year when she won all those merit certificates for every subject and her mum came to school wearing blue eye shadow. There was a special parents' section at the back of the assembly hall but it was empty except for Mrs Worthington, straining her neck and clapping her hands at chin level.

'Victoria Worthington – certificate of merit,' the headmaster had to shout seven times and each time Vicky crossed the stage in a funny speeded up walk with a face like mortification. At the end of the ceremony her mum came up and gave her a poke in the ribs.

'Well done Vicky,' she says. 'Smartie pants all the way. Our very own Wonder Woman.' Vicky's mum is English and she speaks like they do on Coronation Street. Usually Vicky just gives a kind of grunt under her breath and rolls her eyes.

'What if everyone in the front rows could see up my skirt?' she says afterwards in the cloakrooms. 'What if he could see my fat bum?'

'You haven't got a fat bum,' I say. 'Just so long as he didn't see the meat mallet sticking out your knickers.' She gave me a look of horror and then her head tilted back and the laugh came like a sneeze when she remembered it too. In time to the beat of 'I love Rock n Roll' she was hopping from one leg to another on top of her bed spread, hitting her backside with one of those wooden meat mallet things she found at the back of the cutlery drawer. Her bum cheeks were taking a beamer at the sides of her Terri towelling knickers.

'Circulation,' she was shouting. 'It gets the circulation going.' She must've figured that one out for herself cause they didn't mention it in Just Seventeen.

Mostly she just says 'He' or 'Him' but sometimes there are other people around and we have to use the code name HP. It stands for Hunky Phil. One time Vicky's mum shouted through the serving hatch,

'Do any of you ladies fancy a squirt of HP sauce on top of those chips?' I had a mouth full of Coca Cola that almost burst on to the checked table cloth. Vicky had to make up a story that I was allergic to HP sauce.

'Whatever next?' said her mum, chewing her pork chop, 'It just goes to show...' and then she turned to watch the weather on Reporting Scotland.

'I love HP sauce though, don't I?' said Vicky, tilting the bottle and looking at me in a kind of James Bond eyebrow way.

'Oh yeah, you love it Vicky. You just can't get enough of it.'

Now that Hunky Phil has left school to work on his Dad's fishing boat, we hardly ever see him except from a distance. From the corner of Shore Street Vicky was still able to detect his new earring.

'Check it out,' she says, with her hand over her mouth, 'he's got his ear pierced.' She sounded like a football commentator announcing a goal. I thought I could see a wee silver hoop but I wasn't sure.

To keep from getting bored at school, Vicky likes to imagine things about him. She is good at helping me with my physics homework and I am good at helping her imaginings.

'Imagine his bedroom,' she says, 'I bet he's got a Habitat duvet that his mum brought back from Glasgow. I bet it's all soft and clean and smells like Persil Automatic.' She was doodling on the cover of her jotter. Miss McTaggart was still drawing chromosomes on the blackboard so I say, 'Imagine him lying in his bed listening to AC/DC with his hands behind his head and underneath the duvet cover he's only wearing a pair of white boxers.'

'God,' she says, 'Imagine,' and laughs with a shiver like she's cold. The doodles turned into little love hearts.

*

Today when she comes into the shop I have some top class info for her but it is Christmas Eve and we are dead busy. 'Merry Mayhem' Frankenstein calls it as he rubs his hands together. Mostly it is people pouring in off the street with their eyes all screwed up from the wind. I can only talk for a minute and I have to show Vicky the revolting jewellery case at the same time. We lean over the glass and she pretends to point to things that she likes.

'Go on then, spill the Heinz,' she says, not looking at me, not daring to take her eyes off a pair of diamonte earrings. It is like we are secret agents. I decide to get it all out in one go.

'I know what Hunky Phil is getting for Christmas because his mum was in earlier and she bought him new Wranglers *and* a sexy new denim jacket *and* she even bought posh wrapping paper *and* he's going to the Chrissy Disco tonight at the Porthole. For certain.' She is staring straight into my eyes and she looks happy, but it is as if she is scared to smile in case the smile might burst off her face. I keep the jewellery rotating to avoid any suspicion.

*

'Chrissy Disco, Chrissy Disco,' we are singing in her bedroom like it is a football supporters' song. We asked good and early this year and our Mums agreed.

'As long as you stick together,' mine said, 'Your know the rumours about that place.' We did but we had only been to the Porthole once before. We were collecting money in the afternoon for our sponsored cycle and we sneaked a look in the back hall. The famous back hall where Willie McCallum punched the barman and Pamela Forsyth got caught 'at it' with two boys in the men's toilets. And on Monday mornings the older girls would huddle in the cloakrooms and squeal,

'God, the Porthole on Friday night – magic laugh or what?' The senior boys would slag each other, 'Hey Davie, did you get your hole at the Hole?'

'Gonna check my make up?' says Vicky, shining the angle poise on to her face, her eyes squinting in the glare. I scan her face for any smudges of mascara or lipstick. Her skin tinted Clearasil looks like orangey dots.

'Fine,' I say.

'Maybe a bit more Cleary to cover this plook,' she says, leaning in to the mirror and dabbing with her middle finger. I nudge my face beside hers and try some of her lipstick. It's called 'Fiery Temptress' and there is a slight taste of Fairy liquid. She stops dabbing.

'Wooo,' she says, 'It looks good on you.' When I laugh it looks even more weird. Giant cartoon lips out of control. Like it's not me at all.

'I look like that old barmaid from the TV.' Vicky must know who I mean cause she does an imitation of her mum:

'Ooh gals, it's time to put me feet up for The Street.' I start to wipe it off with a tissue.

'Don't be daft,' she says, 'It's nice – honest.'

'Naa,' I say 'Canny be bared.' It's our shorthand for 'I cannot be bothered.'

Before we leave we sneak into her mum's bedroom and spray ourselves with perfume from the dresser. I try *Charlie* and she pumps *Liberty* behind both ears and then down her front. We are sniggering and the flowery scent hits the back of my throat, making me cough.

'Bye Mum,' Vicky shouts from the kitchen, as she opens the back door.

'Aww, come on in and give us a fashion parade first,' her mum yells back over the News at Ten music.

'Sorry, gotta rush,' shouts Vicky, pulling a face at me as we step out into the blustery night. I feel relieved that I don't have to do a twirl while Mr Worthington sucks on his pipe and Vicky's mum says,

'Ooh, gals about town eh? Out in your glad rags tonight.' Then she always says the other stuff. 'Just you watch those boys, Vicky. They're only after one thing and believe me chuck, it's not your brains. You know what your gran always said. If you can't be good be extra, extra careful.'

We can hear the thump of the music as we round the street corner. The windows are filled with condensation and from outside all the Christmas lights look like they have wee halos.

'You go first,' says Vicky.

'No, you.' I say and then I give in, knowing we could spend ages in the cold. I walk a shoulder in front of her but it hits us both in the same moment. Music so loud it tingles all over, like we just jumped into deep water. Warm air, heavy with the smell of smoke and beer and polished wooden floors. I order the cider and the barmaid says nothing. Vicky slips me 50p at thigh level to pay for hers. I think she looks pretty in the low lights with her make up on.

'Seat, seat, seat,' she says through gritted teeth in a kind of false grin and I know we will both feel better if we can find a place to sit down.

'Over there,' I say and we get a corner bench in front of a round table. It's one of those copper ones with the dimpled metal effect and it reminds me of Vicky with the meat mallet, whacking her derriere as she sometimes calls it.

On the dance floor a few of the girls from school are dancing in huddled groups. They look really different here, away from double maths and pack lunches. Sort of glamorous like they're on TV. Gillian Stewart is wearing new stretch Wrangler's and her lips are shiny with lip gloss. Only Jane McKinley looks out of place. Her white bra is glowing luminous beneath a yellow T-shirt under the disco lights. It's one of those big corsety bras like someone's Auntie would wear. Vicky and I smile at each other as if we have just narrowly avoided disaster.

'Oh my God, don't look, don't look, he's here,' says Vicky, staring hard into her lap. I look up and he is standing at the bar with his top lip hovering over a full pint glass. He's wearing a checked shirt with his new denim jacket and jeans and he looks like a cowboy without the hat.

'It's okay,' I say, 'He's staring at the dance floor,' and she allows herself another sneak glance.

'Ohhhh,' she sighs. Like a kind of baby-animal-is-injured sigh.

'He's gorgeous, he's completely and utterly gorgeous. Look at his *hair*. I wish I could remember how to dance.'

'Course you can,' I say. 'Let's wait till the start of the next record.'

I know what she means though. When we walk on the half empty dance floor, I feel as if everyone is looking and suddenly I feel awkward and strange. Like we are astronauts who can't get used to gravity again. She shouts something in my ear, still dancing, her hand swaying like she is beating an invisible egg.

'Yeah,' I shout back, smiling, cause she is smiling and I don't hear what she said. Another record comes on and suddenly I feel happy. I am okay, I can do this stuff too. I like the feel of the music and the feel of my skirt as I'm dancing. I risk a little twirl, and then another. I want to close my eyes and sing the words but I have to stop myself. It is as if I am singing them under my breath. And I have to keep a look out. For us both.

When he asks me to dance, I don't see him coming. I feel a tap on my shoulder and he nods at me, eyebrows raised. Vicky gives me that big wit-tee-woo smile but it doesn't reach her eyes. She sits down, sips her drink and looks into the middle distance as if she is waiting on someone or something.

'How's it goin' up at Alcatraz?' Hunky Phil shouts, leaning in to my ear and I get a breath of after shave. A sort of fresh pine smell.

'Oh, just the usual rubbish,' I say, although I don't mind school. Sometimes in double English I even feel content. Like I want to take my shoes off and get comfy while I watch the rain outside and listen to Mr Dawson's deep voice as he reads Shakespeare. I don't really care if I don't understand it all. I just feel like I'm where I should be. Not like the shop. In the shop I'm scared. Scared of Frankenstein and the customers and scared of getting the till wrong.

'Thank God I've left that dump,' he says. 'I'm saving up for a motor now.' His hoop earring is glinting in the light like those little minnows you see in the shallows.

'Cool,' I shout back, because I can't think of anything else to say but somehow it does seem cool that Hunky Phil who ate the same macaroni in our school canteen would soon be driving around like he was a grown up man. I look across at Vicky and now she is staring straight at me as if I am betraying her with every word. The song is nearly over so I lean in towards his neck and I ask him. I try to make my voice sound light as if it is just a casual inquiry, a light hearted suggestion. Like Frankenstein over the jewellery counter.

'What about this one? Would you like to give it a try Madam?' But he is shaking his head.

'Naaa,' he says. He does not have to explain and I don't want him to either. If Hunky Phil does not want to dance with my friend then that is that.

'Hope you get a car then,' I say and raise my hand in an awkward wave as I walk back to Vicky.

'What was he saying?' She has downed all of her cider during the record.

'Och, nothing much really,' I say. I know there is no point in telling her about the car. This time Vicky goes up to the bar and gets another drink for herself. We sit and sip and I can't think of anything to say. I think of how excited we were earlier and now there is only the flatness of a bad Sunday afternoon. A slow dance record comes on and we exchange 'what now?' looks. A lot of the couples hug in close. Big Alan Johnson is wrapped around Jane McKinley, covering up her luminous bra. His eyes are closed and I look at Vicky for her reaction but she is not playing any more. She is just gazing at the lights and the badly painted sign that says Disco Blue.

I see his hand before I realise it is him. Just these hands clasping the cheeks of a bum in stretch Wranglers and as they turn I see it is Gillian Stewart's bum. It is her shiny hair falling down her back as she tilts her face up to his. And when Hunky Phil kisses her I see a flash of his tongue and it looks greedy and passionate like it does in the movies. I am wondering about the wetness of it all and how it must feel to kiss a boy on top of the lip gloss, or to kiss a boy at all, when I realise that Vicky has left. And then I see her, making her way through the swaying couples, her shoulders drawn in, in case she should touch any of them. Like a dodgem car going the wrong way.

The sign on the toilet door says 'Ladies' and there is a brass propeller above the door frame. One of the sixth form girls staggers out, clutching a drink, her other hand tucking her blouse into her jeans. I push the swing door and inside Vicky is standing before the mirror. The sink in front of her is clogged with wet toilet roll and cigarette ash. Her tears are making her mascara run and her big red lips are quivering and turned down at the corners. For a moment I have a strange thought that if she had a bowler hat and a flower she'd look like one of those cry clowns at the circus. The crap ones that are never even funny. I glance across at the cubicles. One of the doors is half closed but I don't see any feet underneath.

'I can't believe I'm so stupid,' she says, directly at her reflection. Her voice is strangely flat as if she feels that, by this stage, sobs would go to waste.

'You're not stupid,' I say but I don't know how to explain it to her any more than that.

'You're really clever,' I rush in, and she gives a snort just as I know I shouldn't have said it. I go into the open cubicle and yank off an arm's length of pink bog roll. She uses it to wipe the slevers from her nose.

'Why does he have to be so bloody gorgeous?' she asks, dabbing her eyes.

I don't know how to answer her and I am hoping that no one comes in and sees her like this. Through the wall the slow record has ended and Slade are singing

'So here it is Merry Christmas,
Everybody's having fun.
Look to the future now,
It's only just begun.'

'Anyway,' I try, 'I bet he doesn't have a Habitat duvet, and if he does, I bet it smells of fish.' She gives a big sigh and then a watery smile.

'Yeah,' she says, 'like that stink you get down the pier.'

'Yeah, rotten old fisherman smell,' I say.

'Mingin' old cod,' she says.

'Bouffin battered haddock.'

'Fried Scampi from Hell.' And I start to laugh. And she is laughing too and then crying a bit more.

Hugh McMillan

ON THE COAST OF NORTH WEST ENGLAND

Willowherb through ribs of iron fret,
and red flowers of rust.
Grey houses scattered by the wind

plant and bud blunt leaves,
blunt kids, skimming stones on sad beaches
thinking of America,

and the arcades at the end of the world.
Dregg, Flimby, Netherton,
in the armpits of dead factories,

their curtains closed
as the sea lies limp at their doors,
the fog just off shore vague like old nightmares.

In Maryport men from the pubs
lug back chips
as the gulls, mimicking their fathers,

follow the little wake home.

Aonghas MacNeacail

DEATAMACH

mar dhuilleag òrach á snàmh
air sruthan siùbhlach na beatha,
neo-ar-thaing gach comhairle,
rùbain gaoil tromh na fèithean

mar chalman bàn, air sgiath eadar
bil acrach is bil acrach, a giùlan
nam facal dìreach dearbhach,
sona gu bheil e na thosgaire

mar ghrian
a' deàrrsadh air gach latha,
falach no follaiseach,
a' deàrrsadh mar bu dual 's
a' tàladh fàs,
mar ghealach airgid
a thilleas is a thilleas
na dannsa mall –
a dannsa caol, a dannsa leathann,
a tarraing 's a sìneadh
cuain is cridhe

mar shàmhchar làn
na talmhain
mar luasgan lainnireach
sgannach na fairge,
mar ghuirme shìorraidh
nan speur

cho lèir's cho deatamach
gun abrainn riut gur
tu mo ghaol

NECESSARY

as a golden leaf swims
on the fast currents of life,
regardless of warnings,
love's ruby through the veins

as a white dove, in flight between
hungry lip and hungry lip, bears
direct and verifiable words,
glad to be the messenger

as a sun
shines on each day,
hidden or visible,
shining as always and
enticing growth,
as a silver moon
returns and returns
in its slow dance –
its slender dance, its broad dance,
drawing up and laying down
ocean and heart

as the earth's
full silence,
as the glittering shoal-deep
motion of the sea,
as the eternal blue
of the sky

so whole, so necessary
that i should tell you
you are my love

Iain MacPherson

UIBHIREACHD

a' dèanamh air a' chuan
bloigh bheag dheth
eadar Canaigh 's an Cuilthionn
eadar connspaid is caolas gaoil
air nach cuireadh tu uibhireachd
co-dhiù
's an latha ag iarraidh mathanas
bho ghlasadh nam beann
agus Ruma ga dhìon
's ga chuairteachadh fhèin
mar chailleach-dhubh
mu choinneamh masladh
fàsach an t-saoghail

DIFFERENTIATION

making for the sea
a wee slice of it
between Canna and the Cuillins
between controversy and love's strait
that you wouldn't differentiate between
anyway
and the day begging forgiveness
from dusk-brown hills
and Rum defending
and encircling itself
like a nun
faced with the outrage
of this world's emptiness

A' TEANNADH A-STAIGH

gam threòrachadh thar an fheòir
tro choille car tiugh
sìos an rathad gu ruige
làrach làn deanntagan
nach fhaicear aig ciaradh an latha

's chaidh sealltainn dhomh
mar eilthireach fo bhuaidh na dibhe
caisteal fo ghealaich dhuibh
agus baile beag an èisg
thall 's pios air falbh bhon Chaol

gu crìoch àraidh an duine
a' teannadh a-staigh mar bhodach beag maol
mar leanabh bochd
an taic an teine

agus sleamhnachd do choise
na h-acarsaid a-nochd
's ged nach tuit mi
feuchaidh mi co-dhiù

HUDDLING INSIDE

leading me over grass
through rather thick forest
down the road
to a nettle-bound site
not seen at dusk

and I was shown
like a drunken pilgrim
a moon-blackened castle
a small fishing village across the Sound
a fair piece from Kyle

to the particular end of humanity
huddled inside like a bald little old man
like a sick child
cradled beside the fire

and your legs' slipperiness
the harbour tonight
and though I won't fall
I'll try to

AN CANADH TU

an canadh tu
gur ann air a dhol bhuaithe
a tha i
a' toirt nan casan leath'
às an dealbh
a b' àbhaist bhith geur?

an creideadh tu
gur ann ri clachan a chur air càrn faoin na cuimhne
a tha mise
a' gabhail fadachd ri rionnagan tighinn air fàire
's a' spreadhadh mun chost an iar
a' tionndadh nan dreag
a chunnaic màthair Dhòmhnaill Mhòir
ann an eilean mo mhàthar fhèin thar a' chuain
's sgapte ar mairbh na ar beò
nuair a thionndaidheas an Crann Beag na Chrann Mòr
os cionn Chamus Crois?

WOULD YOU SAY

would you say
that she's lost the plot
making tracks
out of the picture
that once was well defined?

would you believe
that I'm busy
paying memory's vain homage
anxious for stars appearing on the horizon
and bursting along the western shores
turning into a death star
caught by Big Donald's mum
in my own mother's land overseas
our dead more scattered than our living
when the Little Plough becomes the Big Plough
somewhere above Camus Cross?

BUS-AISEIG

am bus 's am bàt-aiseig
a' tighinn air fàire
ciaradh an fheasgair
Eàrlais 5.45

mise ris a' bhruthach san Eilean
's tusa air a' chuan à Uibhist

solais a' faicinn sruth
rathad a' leantail stuadh
air mullach bràigh Uige

's nach ann mar sin
a thèid ar beò-ghlacadh
leis a' ghrèin 's leis an uair
ann an dàn nan eileanan iar

feamainn 's thusa
ri buain aig glasadh an latha

FERRY-BUS

bus and ferry
appearing on horizons
dusk
Eàrlais, 5.45

I climbing on Skye
you over the sea from Uist

lights sighting current
road winding wave
high above Uig bay

and isn't that
how we'll be captured
by the sun and the hour
in Hebridean fate

you and seaweed
to reap at the dying of the day

Gordon Meade

I. ELEVEN SEA ANEMONES AND ONE CORAL

Snakelocks	Beadlet	Dahlia
Burrowing	Strawberry	Cloak
Plumose	Gem	Daisy
Parasitic	Jewel	Cup

III. A DOZEN WORMS

Square-tailed	Bootlace	Arrow
Honeycomb	Green Leaf	Keel
Horsehair	Peanut	Parchment
Red Ribbon	Peacock	Scale

V. ELEVEN CRABS AND ONE GOBY

Hairy	Edible	Hermit
Spider	Porcelain	Masked
Swimming	Spiny	Thornback
Velvet	Shore	Black

David Millar

MATES

I've been your mate for fifteen fucking years. I don't know if you want to be *my* mate any more but I'm fucked if I want to be *yours*.

Me and you. You and me. I could sooner divorce Joannie than I could shrug *you* off. A lot of marriages are like this. We don't even *like* each other but we're tied together till death, bound together by congealed innocent blood. You, me and Herod the King. You never got that, when I called you that two Christmases ago. But then, you always were a thick cunt.

Christ, they shouldn't be dead those lassies. There are whole days when I think about *nothing else* except going along to the Cop Shop and saying. 'Look it was me, it was us.' We'd both get put away. You'd get life. Christ knows what I'd get. And what would Joannie and the kids' lives be like?

Where do I figure anyway? Accessory after the fact? Murderer? I held that girl still while you slid a knife into her. God help me, I can't deny it. On the face of it, I'm as guilty as you. I didn't *know*. I *didn't know*.

But I swear on my youngest's head. I thought I was restraining her, keeping her from flying at you, and all the time I was really holding her steady so that you could stick her with that stupid fucking blade.

I tried to say a prayer as the life went, well, wherever it is life goes to when it's done. The only one I could remember was the Lord's Prayer: but it was better than fuck all. Tell *that* to the jury!

Aye, I rocked that dying girl in my arms and muttered 'Our Father, Who art in Heaven...'. But He couldn't have been in that night. You went to the car, stabbed the other one and did fuck knows what to her while she was dying. You were gone a good while; she took a long time to die that lassie. I thought you'd gone to calm her down. Well – you did that all right.

That night, I'd had a row with Joannie. I can't even remember what about now. Probably some shite about money. We were always fighting about money then. So, down to 'The Clover Leaf', sharp-angled, simmering, the veins at my temples swollen with the blood pounding through them. There was a guy there, I knew a wee bit, who was selling covers from kids' downies. They were probably nicked but I bought one for wee Mark anyway. It was a Wednesday night, a quiet night. I didn't want to talk to anyone really. And probably not *you* given the choice. The word in the pub was that you were a headbanger, but then I've always taken a pride in not listening to guys in pubs. And we'd worked together once. Not for long, because you got your jotters after two and a half weeks. And what the fuck was all *that* about anyway. But we were apprentices at MacCutcheon's the joiners together. And you were a quiet wee guy then; I remember you sitting there with a can of juice and your sandwiches wrapped up in an old creased white paper bag. We were surprised when you just disappeared.

And we started yacking, the way you do. Half pints and nips. You had a new motor, a Capri. Did I fancy going into town? Did I fancy going into *town*? Why not? It was either that or stay in 'The Clover Leaf'. Or trudge home to spend the evening fighting with Joannie in between Coronation Street and Dallas. I remember what it was we were fighting about now. She was pregnant for the fourth time since we were married. I just couldn't see where the money was to come from.

That wean's not far off the age those two lassies were back then. She keeps asking to go out, into town. But I know (who better) that there'll be some flash cunt like you, with a fat wallet in one pocket and a big knife in another. So I rage at her and she storms and sulks. She goes to Joannie and we all start fighting and I can never tell them why not.

Aye, some flash cunt like you with a wad of notes and your patter out the Old Testament.

I saw them giggling when you were chatting them up. When you asked them if they'd like a ride down to the beach at Gullane, I thought they'd laugh in your face. Two eighteen year olds sitting with a couple of guys in their thirties, one with a fat belly and a beer stained face and the other dressed in the fashions of the Nineteen-Sixties. Lucky that the pub was busy. Lucky everyone was involved in their own business. If it'd been half-full or there'd been a few nosy bastards there, the Police would've picked us up the next morning. A *cherry-red corduroy trouser suit*, for fuck's sake: you stood out like a Christmas cracker in July. Instead, when I saw the identikit pictures, I almost cried with relief.

I sometimes imagine lives for those lassies. In the wee hours, when the kids are asleep and Joannie's snuffling and snuggling into me, I imagine lives for those lassies. Different ones, probably more exciting than they would've led. One worked behind a bar and the other was a teller in a bank. I give them rich husbands, good jobs and nice houses in the suburbs of a city that doesn't exist. I give them holidays all over the world; but I never put them on a beach now. I did it a couple of times but *you* always appear with a slack and gummy old man's smile.

And your knife.

You've always got a knife.

It was high jinks all the way out of the city. But they began to quieten down when you started the heavy sexual innuendo. I did my best to lighten things up, but they can sense these things, women. And they probably didn't trust me either, probably wondered why I was trying to calm things down. They didn't ask you to let them out the car. Can you blame them really? Bible black, drizzle hissing off the car's body, the middle of nowhere and a long haul back to the city.

If I could live that night over again, I'd dunt you on the head with the fucking wheel brace until you stopped the car and let them out. To freedom. To freedom and a few callouses; but they'd've had their lives.

It was Dirleton we ended up at, not Gullane at all. Did you figure that? Did you reckon there'd not be much happening at that time of night? You parked the car in a wee car park there and we all sat and listened to the silence. There weren't any other cars or other people and I wasn't very sure if I could hear the sea or not. I thought it might be all right then, because the silence wasn't the embarrassed kind. It was an easy silence, the silence of four friends who'd had a couple of drinks and were going to have a stroll along the beach before turning in. I was only *thinking* in terms of embarrassment then. I was thinking you'd probably try and get off with one of them, the dark haired one in the passenger seat, and it was going to be an embarrassment for me and the other lassie, whether you succeeded or not. When you suggested to her that the two of you should go and look at the sea, it was kind of a relief. Oh, you bastard, telling her to take your jacket to keep the cold out.

You let yourself out and went around to the passenger door to let the lassie out, true gentleman that you are. As the door closed, I turned to the blonde lassie and shrugged. She started to ask me what I worked at. I didn't have time to say anything before I heard you shouting.

I didn't see you for a week or so after it. 'The Clover Leaf' again. Another row with Joannie. We'd rowed every night for a week, always over nothing: I'd forgotten to do this: I'd spent too much dough in 'The Clover Leaf'; wee Paul needed another pair of shoes.

Well, they aren't nothing really these things. They used to be important in the kind of life I used to live. But having a lassie sobbing her life out in your arms kind of puts things into a brutal perspective.

You bought me a whiskey and a half pint and pulled me over to the table where the scorer usually sits during the darts matches. I couldn't look you in the eye. You reached over and put your hand on my arm. I shook it off and you told me to take it easy.

I got the impression during that conversation, and others over the next couple of years, that you felt I should look up to you. Look up to you. Look up to *you*. That somehow, you'd grown in stature and become a very impressive human being indeed. Someone to be reckoned with. It took two or three years for it to dawn on you that I'd gladly have ground my tumbler in your face. And you must have realised what bound us.

You asked me if everything was all right. Had I said anything to anyone? Of course I hadn't. You said that the descriptions in the papers were nothing like us. And you laughed. As if all you'd done was nick a packet of fags off a shop counter. As if it was all just a game between us and the Police. Butch Cassidy and the Sundance Kid. Except they didn't slaughter a pair of lassies in their prime.

And after that, you'd always join whatever company I was in. You'd give the impression that we had important things to talk about and people took the hint. After a year or so, every-one began to see us as mates. By then I was anxious in *their* company and I didn't like *yours*. Their conversation is about pale ghostly things, from another life, from another planet. The things *you* talk about make no sense and we spend a lot of time sitting side by side in silence. I suppose we are mates in a way; we've both been feared that one of us would say something out of turn. Take a drop too much and spill our guts.

There was the time, five years ago, when one of the Sunday papers did one of those articles about unsolved crimes. There was you, me, Foley and Larry. Larry sitting there saying hanging's too good for those cunts, whoever they are, and you nodding sagely like a High Court Judge.

You never came round to the house. Why not? You always 'phone. Would the sight of my teenage lassies maybe start you thinking. Maybe have you wondering what colour the Hell their folks' lives has been all this time. I'll tell you, Joannie and me had a stillborn wean, a long time back, and that's enough grief for anyone's lifetime.

But I reckon they cut out your conscience when you were young. Now and then, I've got the idea that you'd do it again. That you'd grown so cocky with never having been caught that you'd like to do it again. Well count me out pal. My life's destroyed, my life runs on different tracks to anyone else's and a blood sacrifice won't save it. When you make those jokes about the younger lassies that come into 'The Clover Leaf' at the weekend, I could choke you where you sit.

From where I was sitting in the car, trick of the light, trick of the dark, it somehow looked as if *she* was going for *you*. I pushed open the car door and ran over. I pinned her arms to her sides and held her in a firm grip, like an executioner's apprentice, while you reached inside your jacket and pulled out your stupid big knife. You stabbed her quickly. She didn't make a sound but I felt the strength going out of her like air out of a balloon. I'll remember that girl dying until the day that I go and the hellish noises coming from the car

What was it you said? I'll take care of the other one. What was that supposed to mean?

Stop her getting hysterical?

Stop her screaming?

No. Stop her life. And do fuck knows what while she's dying. I heard the thick curdling scream of panic, fear and outrage coming from the car. To die that young. And at the hands of a waster like you.

Sometimes, I hear her screaming 'Help me, help me,' but I'm not sure if that really happened. You've never told me exactly what you *did* do while you were with her in the car; there are some lines even *you* won't cross.

I think sometimes that I'll never be at peace until one of us is dead and, I admit, in my mind, I've killed you many times over. I couldn't see *me* doing it, but I sometimes wonder if *you* could. I stagger out of here many a night scarcely knowing the hour and it wouldn't take much to put me away. But I don't think you would.

There's a part of you needs at least *one* other human being to know what you've done. All right. What *we've* done. I'm as fucking guilty as *you*. And then, I seem to be your only mate in the world. That's why we're in each other's company so much. We're manacled together for the rest of our naturals and we'll each stay close to the other because *I* need to make sure that you keep your mouth shut and *you* need someone to share your glory. Christ though, it's a high price to pay for being alive.

And when it was done. When one of them was lying in my arms all relaxed, all floppy and bloody, and the other one had stopped screaming, we had to tidy up. I was like a robot, I did exactly what you said.

I can see some guy in a wig saying, 'Didn't you think of calling the Police?' and the answer is no, at no point did I think of calling the Police.

You issued orders like a drill sergeant and I obeyed them in a trance, with dulled eyes, stiff face, thoughts still as a stinking stagnant pond. I only came alive when you opened the boot and fished out the new downie cover I'd bought for wee Mark. I yanked it away from you and you told me we needed it. To make it look like a sex crime, you said. Sometimes, oh, sometimes, you have to laugh. Make it *look* like a sex crime. As if anyone with a full set of fuses was going to think anything else. But you said no, we've got to make it look like it was a couple of weirdos. We tore the material into strips and gagged and bound the two lassies. I had to close the blonde one's eyes; she wouldn't stop staring at me. They were this pale pale blue.

Where the fuck *was* everyone that night?

Where were all the nosy bastards walking their dogs?

The teenagers out for a bit of nookie in the old man's car?

If we'd been caught then I would've seemed exactly what I was; a man in a state of extreme shock, as fragile and malleable as newly blown glass.

But the further time's slipped on from that night, the bigger my share of the blame grows and one day my head'll open and spew a porridge of bloody brains and black guilt over the town.

You took the car as close to the beach as you dared and we left them, trussed up, not like anything human any longer, not like anything that anyone had ever cherished or loved or given a fuck about; we left them beside a litter bin that had ice cream wrappers, bits of hamburger rolls and chip papers overflowing from it.

The door opens and here you come. My mate. My mucker. My marra. Already, I'm signalling Bobby behind the bar to pour another pint and I wonder for the four thousandth time why I don't just say:

'Fuck off out of it. Fuck off out of my life, you scum.'

But it's too late for that. It's been too late every day for the last fifteen years.

William Neill

THE CAULD WUND O THE NICHT

(Frae the French o Leconte de Lisle 1818–1894)

Cauld thro the brainches souchs the wund o nicht — *sighs*
An aa the while the dry sprots brak an faa — *twigs*
The deid sleep on the muirland under snaw
Lik deid-claes happit roon thaim, lang an bricht. — *shrouds, wrapped*

On the faur easin's mairch a streik o black, — *horizon's edge*
The lang flicht o the craws alang the grunn
Whaur dugs are scartin on a knowe abune — *dogs scratching, knoll above*
Fechtin ower banes skailt in the coorse wrack. — *Bones scattered, coarse grass*

Doun in the broozilt girse I hear thaim grane, — *crushed grass,*
O nicht's gash indwallers wha ryse nai mair — *pale*
whit wersh remembrance steirs yir saucht doun thare — *bitter, stirs your peace*
Ti caa frae stivvent lips sic wechtie main? — *frozen, heavy moaning*

Ye maun forleit! Yir hairts are muildert nou; — *must forget, mouldered*
Aa yir lang veins are cauld an tuimt o bluid — *emptied of blood*
O creagh o aiver duans, ye couthie deid, — *prey of ardent verses, happy*
Mynd on yir lives an soonder sleep ablo. — *Remember, sounder, below*

Ah, whan I jyne ye doun in yon deep lair — *join, grave*
Like ti a slave when age has lowsed his chynes, — *freed, chains*
Bien I sal ligg, weill redd o leivin's pynes, — *comfortable, lie, rid, living's pains*
Hou blythe again gae doun ti stour yince mair. — *dust, once more*

A dwaum. The deid byde quaitlie in thair nicht, — *dream, remain silent*
Ainlie the wund, the fyke o seekin dugs; — *only, scrabble*
Fell nature's dowie air ower aathing liggs, — *doleful, everything*
Athin ma ain wersh hairt this skaith an blicht. — *harm and blight.*

Haud aff! The lift is deif, the yird disdains, — *hold back, sky, earth*
Whit sairves ti greet ower whit ye canna mend? — *weep*
Yon deidlie dunt will quait ye in the end; — *deathly blow, quiet*
Wha bites daith's dirk maun eftir dree his blains. — *suffer his wounds*

Yince mair a pyne, yince mair anither clour,   pain, blow
Then nocht. Yird gants ti haud a puckle flesh.   Nothing, earth gapes, morsel
Girse disna mynd on ocht, but green an nesh   Grass, remember, anything, tender
Growes whaur life's vanitie liggs evermair.

Tom Pow

MY FATHER'S FUNERAL

It's the first frosty day in November,
a day pure as a walk along Dornoch beach,
when all the brush strokes are clear – each wave
of sand, of sea, each twirl of wispy cloud –
and your nose to the canvas all the way
to Embo. 'Bonnie.' Aye, bonnie right enough.
Today though, it's the Pennines I cross
to reach you: they lapping, silver on green,
below a sky *you'd* call 'cerulean blue' –

it's almost a shock, dad, the day's
painted with such a full palette.
Then, arriving at the first staging post
to the grave, in the close family hubbub,
it's no surprise to find you not there,
preferring instead a private moment's
vanity in the long hall mirror, rubbing
your moustache with delight at how black
suits you – you and those flashing brown eyes!

Later, as we wait beside the sleek hearse
for *Agnes*, you go walkabout again –
an absence you can conjure anywhere
(the tuneless whistle, the stamping dance) –
caught between contemplation of your shoes
and the waiting of a man at the end
of a million accumulated waitings,
a man who can't possibly wait longer –
till, 'Ah, here she comes now. *Michty me*! –

what kept her?' addressing a top-hatted
pall-bearer, his northern accent so rich,
the gravity of the occasion flies from us
and we share a conspiratorial wink.
It's after, I catch you glancing across
at the grave-diggers, leaning on their shovels
under bare oak trees, sharing a joke,
their job half done. And that's where I think
you'd like to be now, anticipating

the punchline, or simply watching them
handle a spade. Country boy at heart,
how you loved to watch anybody
do something well. But, suddenly it's over:
the singing, the prayers, and the tears.
                                                        You're last
to leave your graveside, turning away,
just when the copper sun angles itself
to perfection; picks out your brass nameplate
and our first scatterings of dry earth.

THE CARD PLAYERS

After the luxury of advocaat, lapped
from one-shot glasses held like nuggets
in our fists, we cluster round the orange light
of the paraffin lamp as the cards are dealt.

For a few nights after my aunt and uncle
have left, we'll play on: Sweaty Betty mostly.
Mum loves to say the name. It's terrible!
Like those other words that have escaped

from *Down Below* where language is fiery
or viscous. We are not, I don't think,
a Games Family but play the hands out
as our heavy reading chairs hunker

in the darkness and the lamp's flame
creeps up till a black feather of smoke
presses itself against the glass funnel.
Between hands I make the shortest walk

to the blind gable end of the cottage.
From here ferns thicken to a real darkness
though the track is still held by light swells
of broom. I piss on the grass; my soft

ssh blurring with the steady burr
of the burn. The stars thicken also –
teased out wool caught on the barbs
of their constellations. For a moment

I'm giddy. When I walk back round
I glimpse the card players past the thin
print curtains; their backs are almost black,
their open faces cut like diamonds

in the lamplight. My cards lie face down
on the table, waiting for me to play them.
Beside them, my father stands, tightening
the top of a hot water bottle.

Richard Price

Flightpaths

Cormorants at the gravel pits,
gannets on a skerry.
Pelicans by the condo boards,
parakeets in Sidney?

More birds flew out
from the SS Pricey –
scuttled on a dryish patch
to start a family –
than those in a flap
in the old dove and raven story.

(The black and white telly
dreamed in colour,
a dream with a logo for a rainbow,
a charter,
and where's the remote?)

Back to the boat.
You could say Mrs Noah died,
and all her birds of paradise
got work in the colonies,
or thereabouts.
Noah, too.

Mum, and Dad, is that not you?
The ungainly creatures, migrated brothers?

'Keep close, will you – promise me that.'

In each less and less makeshift flat
even the phone's a kind of bird.
Grip it by the head,
hold the chest and prod.
Connect what's left
of the flightpaths of the world.

Suhayl Saadi

BANDANNA

To Ustad Nusrat Fateh Ali Khan

He had been dusting for nearly half-an-hour but it felt like his whole life. The shop was becoming unbearably warm. Its lemon walls were beginning to crowd in on him, so that he felt soon he would be crushed beneath their dull, yellow weight. The air was stifling, dead and yet he seemed to need great gulps of it. He felt that he would begin to expand like an overfed goldfish and would burst through the shelves, the plaster, the broken clock. He forced his right hand to continue wiping dust off the mica counter while with his left, he adjusted the knot of his bandanna. Somewhere at his back, his parents busied themselves as they always had, all their lives. Busy, busy, busy.

The sounds of running and shouting shifted from the street in through the open doorway, disturbing the suffocating rhythm of the morning. Plastic on tarmac. Spittle. The big sky. Sal recognised the voices, and his heart leapt, then felt empty. As the lads ran past the burning glass, Salman Ishaq allowed the duster to fall from his hand. He watched it cut a delicate, slightly imperfect trajectory through the methi air and then ran out of his father's shop to shrieks of

Haraam zaada! Five minutes work, and he's done? Hud haraam. Useless bastard!

They did not beckon, entreat or threaten him to come back; he knew this was because they would not expect him to have listened. He knew, as the sun's heat embraced his ears, burning out the fading, effervescent cries of home that during the succeeding minutes, hours, years his father would accuse his mother of having brought defective genes into the family, and his mother would retort to her majaz-i-Khuda, the life of her heart, that it would not have been possible to pollute the blood of his people, since their blood had already been dirtier than a Muzaffarabad cesspool. Love among the peasants was like that, mused Salman Ishaq (or 'Sal', as he was known outside of his home and his hundred-strong brathery, though his parents and all of the aunties remained in total ignorance – blissful, perhaps – of this almost Roman and hence porcine nickname). He slackened his stride, allowing his long, Reebok'd legs to spring up

and down on the quivering asphalt. White on black. Sal was
fair-skinned, almost white – in any other country except
Caledonia he would've been white, say Italy for example, or
Espana or Portugal, or Greece or… he cursed his luck for ending up in this country of wallpaper-blond people. He cursed his
parents. Fuckin ignorant peasants. Knew how to milk a coo
and shit in the fields (and, he admitted begrudgingly, how tae
run a Carry-out Off-licence) but when it came to knowin
where they were at, he chuckled with a thoroughly blond glee,
they didnae have a clue, no fuckin clue. The group of lads he
was following were also running, though not as fast and so he
was able tae cover the ground rapidly and would soon be up
with them. After aw, that wis why he had dropped his duster in
the first place (an in several other places, too) symbol as it wis
ae servitude fuck, he wisnae hovin that, his fellow-gang mem-
bers seein him mop a fuckin flaer. No way. In the distance, their
bandannas darted up and down, dun specks amid the gleaming
bodies of cars. They were weaving in and out, darting between
the moving vehicles, making them stop altogether at times, and
then they'd be up onto the pavement and then back into the
swim of the road. He could hear their shouts and the curses of
the motorists, and began to feel the pulse in his chest grow
stronger, impelling him to join then, to orgasm in vandal with
the gang. Some of the drivers were shouting through rolled-
down glass, swearing in Punjabi as well as in English, both at
his pals up ahead and now also at him, too, as he began darting
in diamond formation, following in the hot tracks of the gang.
Halfway down Albert Drive, he caught up with his comrades,
and slapped Ali on the shooder.

'Hey, bhen-chaud! What's up?' Ali shouted in smiles.

They exchanged Bronx palm-slaps while from beneath the
thick waves of August heat, a bass guitar thudded epileptiform
rhythms, Bombay Dopplersahb spirals from an open-topped
sportscar.

Thunk!
Roo-roo-roo-roo-roo
Love me!
Thunk!
Roo-roo-roo-roo-too
Love me!

They started off again, the three of them, impelled by the
insistent thrum of the music in their ears. As the Gang ran on,

the shopkeepers moved in glue, hardly noticing them as they whooped past. They lived in a different time, another place. The dhokandaars were strung on the drone of a sarod, they pulsed to the rhythms of a different beat, a beat of the seasons, of the peasant calendar, of monsoon into dry and dry in monsoon. They knew nothing of white water, or of white women. They slunk along the fields of their gao's, happy only to be a little more than serfs. They asked for nothing else. Would have seen it as presumptuous, in another man's country. Sal felt a buzz in his brain. He was on the runnin-board, and they were pedestrians.

They reached the end of the street. Ahead lay the Tramway, a theatre which none of them had ever been in, not even when the Mela had been there. The Mela wis jis fur kids and cooncillurs. Sal and his dosts preferred machines to people. They were noisy, irascible, silicon-based like Michael Jackson. They'd play the robots for hours, not bothering whether they won or lost, not caring about the game. Just moving into the beat of chip upon chip, a twitch of the film-star thigh, the hot shoulder shuffle. They were on the film-set, they were living in total. There were no spaces in their existence. No gaps of silence. The Gang turned west, away fae the Mosques, towards Maxwell Park. That's where they were heidet. To the pond, and the trees. To muck up the quiet. To fill it wi gouts ae Bhangra and Bassie. They skatit past the tenement closes, each one a blink in the Gang's eye. The sound of generations carved into each corniced ceiling. Flip back: Sal, in the gao. Or, to be more accurate, in Azaad-Kashmir, the Land of Freedom. His family's land, earth-brown like their skins (not like Sal's, though), old blood, like the tenement stone. But Sal was another kind of Azaadi. Another hybrid. His was a freedom-within-freedom. A distant, grainy monochrome of greased colonials. Sal, formed between the dots of white and black, somewhere in the invisible alchemical mix flooding through the paper. Long before his conception, Sal was there in the deep line of Partition, in the slime cartridge hate of the one for the other. Peel back the layer, the snakeskin deceptions of Poonch, now in the Occupied Kashmir previously in Dogra-land, before that, a gleam in the eye of the Great Mughal, and back, beyond the photo frame, through the nastaliq of dynasties, swimming through the hot sperm of a thousand, to Sikander, Conqueror of the World. Fast-forward: Sal an The Gang. The Black Bandannas. Black,

because it made their faces look whiter. Italian, almost. Or
Spanish, or Portuguese, or anything. As a pose tae the Kinning
Park boys. As opposed tae...
        The Uni-bastards
        The Mosquers
        The Khans
        and The Rest.
They were all small-time, forming and disbanding from one
year to the next in tenuous hierarchies of slang ad spittle.
Transient allegiances like in the Games, the video-shop computer games. Nothing was static. Life was movement, juddering,
twitching, filmi-star movement. Peasant to refugee, refugee to
kisaan; emigrant to immigrant, Paki tae dhokandaar; shopkeeper tae gang-member. Sal slowed to a walking pace. The
swagger of the multitudes. Zafar lit a cigarette, handed the pack
roon. Puffin draws, they got their breath back.
        'Where're we gan?' Ali asked. Ali wis a Shia. Less than a
human being, according tae the shitfaced cunt in the Bookshop.
        'The Park,' Zafar replied, brusquely.
        Ali curled his lip.
        'The Park's borin. Ah dinnae want tae go thir.'
        'You shut the fuck up, arsehole.'
        Ali shut up. He knew his place in the Gang, and that was
as its arsehole. Zafar was its head, its brains, its brigadier
(unlike Pakistan, the gangs did not have more brigadiers than
sergeants).
        'What'll we do there? In the Park.' Sal asked, measuring his
words, levelling them down into the shape of an unobtrusive
wheatfield.
        'Sit, smoke, watch the burds. Tear the trees doon.'
        'Tear the trees? What the fuck for?'
        'Why the fuck not?'
        Sal shrugged. Zafar was a line ae crack on black. Clear-cut
and paagal. Sal wished he could be like that. As they walked
along Darnley Street, Sal spotted a group of girls approaching
from the opposite direction. They were growing like breasts,
and he recognised wan ae his cousins amongst them and began
tae hurl abuse as soon as he thought they might be within
earshot. Not before. There was nothin more embarrassin than
swearin at someone, and they couldnae fuckin hear you. The
girls did hear it, and flung it right back, and the interchange
continued as the two groups passed each other as though

through a mirror and moved gradually out of earshot again. She had long, black hair, his cousin and he watched her swing it as she swore. Swung it around legs which he had never seen, but which he had often imagined as long, sinuous, soft, enticing... Fuckin bitch. He watched her as she disappeared around the corner. An imprint on his eyelids, and an ache in his groin. He blinked, and she was gone. But not the ache. The swollen throbbing expanded like Pakistan from the 'plane, and became a marriage ceremony. A man-in-a-mask, the elephant's vision. A bride, weeping tears through a warranteed hymen.

Ali jabbed him in the ribs. Raised his thick, black eyebrows.

'Randy bastart.'

'No way. No fuckin way, man.'

Ali shook his head, his lop-sided, peasant's skull.

'When the time comes...'

'It'll nivir come.'

'Nae mair white burds, wi thur wide open cunts askin fur it, a glais ae vodka an their yours, nae matter how black ya are. Jis feed them enough booze and dope, and they'll screw you and thank you fur it.'

'At least ah get them.'

That shut him up, Ali. Him, wi his big bug eyes. Too big. They saw too much. They'd get him intae trouble, wan ae these days. Parso, they'd fuck him up, doon an sideeways. He remembered a thin white cow he'd screwed last month. The feel ae her anorexic thigh-joins. Bone on bone. Jag-mairks. They'd huv tae be stoned tae fuck a Paki. And then, only fur blue-backs. He began tae harden. Hated himsel. Puffed on his ciggie. It had gan oot.

'Goa match?' he asked Zafar.

Zafar didn't answer.

Silent bastart, thought Sal and he flung the ciggie doon, killin its corpse wi a stroke ae his trainer.

You'll smoke your life away his mother had said. So many fuckin times. Like, they nivir said onyhin original, like there wis nuhin new in them. Nivir hud been. Jis work, work an work, like it wis the only thing in life. Kaam, kaam, kaam. Fuckin peasants. He wisnae in that trap. Gangstas were ootside ae aw that crap. They were on the border. Alang the silent razor. Between the dots, Sepia, again. Short-haired men with wives. Babies, dead-already. Visions of the past, of past lives. A long, Hindu cacophony. Sal laughed, inside of himself. He

would never be born as a shopkeeper. Better, a dog. At least
you got tae fuck freely. Or a mullah. Just sit in the mosque, and
take money. Blue-backs. Grow a beard and never, ever smile.
An easy job, really. One day, maybe. An image of a large bon-
fire. The Gangs, all throwing their bandannas into the flames.
Black, red, blue. Even the Kinning Park Boys. All sprouting
long, gray beards and adopting a bow-legged walk. The bon-
fire spread, and burned away the image.
      And what's behind it?
      Sal the Gangsta asked Salman Ishaq Sahb the Mohlvi.
      Wagging his well-muscled finger, Ishaq Sahb gave the
answer.
      Behind every image, there is always a jagirdaar. Just as (he
went on) *in ever Coca-Cola tin there is a naked Amirkan slut,
her legs overhanging the metal...*
      OK, OK Sal the Gangsta cut in, a little embarrassed, *but
what about ma Irn Bru tin?*
      The Mullah did not understand. In England, all tins were
the same, he intimated. Just being a tin, was enough. More than
enough. Just thinking about a can might even be sufficient.
      But how could he know, Sal thought, unless he too, had
been there, into the metal between the jag-scarred thighs of the
slut and had swum around (beard, frown-and-all) in the great
fizzy vacuum of the West. Of Amrika, of Glasgee. The mullahs
were all Amrikan agents. See-Eye-Aye. Everyone knew that.
Even his father knew that, fur fuck's sake.
      Now they were passin the Safeway, an there the pretty cars
aw row'd up like obedient schoolkids. Only they weren't
learnin onyhin. The Great White Superstores, stolid bastions
thrown in a ring aroon the city. His father often railed against
the toilet-friendly conglomerates, saying that they'd milk the
small shopkeeper dry. *And what did loag want, Khuda-ke liye,
a local, living-room sized dhokaan with you know a friendly
face, or a giant metal aircraft hanger? What was the future of
our people in this country?* He sounded like a guardian of the
tiny units of commerce with Bonaparte had faced, ranged in
bared teeth shopfronts along the white, Doverine cliffs of Albert
Drive. And they were the new Napoleons, the massive brick
battleships, the Safeways, the Sainsburys, the ASDAS besieging
Glasgee, attacking Scola, runnin thur damned South American
produce right intae the khanas of his ane bratherie. Apples ae
Shaitan. The Gang chased past the trees of knowledge which

burgeoned in the spacey grounds of the Hutcheson's Grammar Schule, the in-vitro incubator of budding intellectuals. Where any parents who needed their kids as fuel for the already bulging middle classes that stuck society together sent their offspring. So many went there, and fucked up. Cause they'd rather rave, than save. Salman had never aspired to a hood-and-gown. Maybe it was his parents' fault. Their lack of ambition. They'd rather he worked in the shop. But then wasn't everything their fault? Comin here in the first place. Runnin a fuckin Paki-shop. That wis that they were seen as. Could've worn top hat an tails, an owned half the city, and they'd still have been Pakis. He hated it. Never, never wanted to be a shopkeeper. Had missed out on learnin. Jis wanted tae be in a Gang, and tae shout. Tae scream in blood and bhangra.

Boom-thaka-thaka-thaka-thaka-thaka
Boom-thaka-thaka-thaka-thaka-thaka
Boom-thaka-thaka-thaka-thaka-thaka

The harsh, Jullundri consonants cut his flesh in slashes of kirpaan; it felt good; upon their blade would his skin grow callused, hard. Nothing would hurt him. No words. No actions. Sticks and stones would shatter on his body. And still he would sing-dance the juddering figure beat, the blood music of exile. The black slaves had bled blue: R 'n' R, hip-hop, reggae; and now the sons of Swastika-daubed Paki-shop owners would disembowel the air in syncopation. Together, with night torches, they would fire the Swastikas and in the fractured air, would spin them round in great wheels up and down the streets of Glasgow. And they would feed the skinheads of Ibrox, the white trash tattoo of Penilee into the great, burning cunt of Mata Kali where five thousand firewheels spun time. Hindu symbols – yes! His parents would have been mortified to hear him thinking that way. But fuck it. They couldnae hear him thinking, no ony mair. It wis aw mixed up, onyway. Sikh Bhangra, Mussalmaan Qawal, Hindu Raag-Bhajan-Khayals… Black Blues, it all swirled together and spumed into a river of Techno-Rave Brummie Beat. And the Gang would rubber-dance in the Victorian park among the trees, the ducks, the water, the shouts of children. Amidst the summer leaves, they would make music, and war.

They leapt over the jagged fence and into the Park. The smell of grass, cut skin-short. Roses like the lips of courtesans, drawing out the sex act into a stream of notes.

Meri naam Jaan-ki bai hai
Meri naam Gauhar Jaan
They half-ran down an incline and tumbled together in a
heap near the bottom. Mothers were pushing prams, the
wheels of which always seemed to go uphill. Children played
with small boats and old folk simply sat in lines on the benches,
as though waiting their turn. Salman closed his eyes. Goldfish
noises...
He felt a fist in his belly, enough to provoke but not to seriously wind him. He turned, and caught another on the jaw. His
head buzzed as he threw his arms outward to grapple with his
opponent. Got a hold of his waist, and didnae let go. Salman
and Zafar wrestled on the grass, rolling and screaming. Ali
leapt in, and his extra weight had the effect of pressing down
on Salman's chest so that he wasn't able to move, and could
hardly breathe. Was not able to say, *Enough's enough, lads.*
Get aff noo. Wasn'y sure they would've listened, anyway. The
sun was streaming into his eyes and he could feel its golden
brilliance flood through the coils of his brain. He could hear
time run backwards through the veins of trees, moving always
anti-clockwise in a broad tape-loop.

In the begi-h-ning, in the begi-h-ning...	C
Every so lo-lo-lo-lo-lo-lonely	C
Chunni uddae uddae jae, guth kul kul jae	C
It is not dying, it is not dying...	C
Kinna Sohna tainu, Rub nay banaya	C
Meri avaaz sunno, mujhe azaad karo	C
Achintya bheda bheda Tattva	C
	C

Turn off your mind, relax and float downstream...

And Salman Ishaq was floating in tears of noor.
Allah-hu
Allah-hu
Allah-hu
Inhale *Allah* Exhale *Hu*
Inhale *Allah* Exhale *Hu*
Inhale *Allah* Exhale *Hu*
Inhale *Allah* Exhale *Hu*
He realised he was able to breathe again. His neck felt stiff.
They had got off his chest and were lying, breathless, beside

him. They were basking in the sun's warmth (this too, would've been unthinkable), half-watching the delicate slivers of light pour down on the park. They had noticed nothing. Would not have cared. They were true Gangstas. For a moment, he felt a rush of pride in being a part of the Black Bandannas – soon, he too, would be capable of feeling nothing – but it passed and left him empty. He looked away from them and just lay there, letting the backs of his fingers rest upon the short, fine blades of grass. The sun filled his eyes, making them sting and water but he did not allow the lids to close. He began to grow blind and it occurred to him that one day, not too far in the future, it would be his fingers that would be pushing up the grass and that what he thought, felt, did, created during that minuscule pause in his fate might live beyond him, his family, the tribe to which he happened to belong and that the one constant in the whole of Maxwell Park – the trees, the birds, the water, the kids – the only beat that pumped all other rhythms, was the beat of love. Salman took a deep breath, the deepest he'd ever taken, it filled parts of his lungs which had never before breathed, not even at the moment of his birth. He felt a great swell of happiness explode infinitely slowly from the centre of his being. His love spread across the grass, the trees, the trunks of dead elephants and returned to him sevenfold

And in the end,
The love you take
Is equal to
The love
You make

The drone behind it all was the note, C, right there in the soul of his brain. He felt its smooth curves, the walls of a tunnel on the way to heaven. And there it was, in the very coils of paradise. He followed a bird as it coursed along the sky. He sat up. Ripping off his bandanna, he ran his finger through his long hair. Felt free. Wanted to leap into the pond, and swim. Desired the cool, green gown of its depth. From far across the city, Salman heard the Azaan carried upriver on currents of music. Rolling his bandanna out onto the grass, he faced towards Gorbals Cross and began to pray.

Glossary

Azaad-Kashmir	Free Kashmir
bhen-chaud	sister-fucker
brathery	blood relatives
dkokaan	shop
dhokandaar	shopkeeper
gao	village
haraam zaada	bastard
hud haraam	useless person (literally, 'bad bones')
jagirdaar	big Punjabi landowner
Jullunder	city in (Indian) Punjab
khanas	rooms
Khuda-ke-liye	for God's sake!
Kisaan	farmer
mela	festival
methi	fenugreek
paagal	crazy
parso	the day after tomorrow
Sikander	Alexander

Adrian Salmond

CYCLISTS

In houses with red curtains
we will lie in till the afternoon
get up, watch videos

later I will scrub your back
in enamel bathtub

and tomorrow
by signposts reading
200 yds subway
cyclists dismount
I will wait for you

Christine M. Stickland

FRIDA KAHLO COMES TO DINNER

Frida Kahlo has come to dinner,
Late, as usual, a little drunk, as usual,
Scattering fag ash like confetti,
Partnered by her perpetual pain
Whose grim claws she wears as lightly
As the ribbons on her dress.
Undefeated, her thirst for life unquenched,
There is more energy in her hair
Than in my entire body.
The brass band of her beads and bangles
Transforms her limping steps
Into a fiesta dance, all rainbow skirts
And flashing teeth and eyes.
Frida Kahlo has come to dinner,
Though eating frankly bores her,
Gets in the way of talking, drinking,
Smoking, painting, making love.
Aware of this, I give her tiny pastries,
Olives, nuts, morsels of spiced meat;
Fuel for her flame, swallowed without tasting.
Frida Kahlo has come to dinner
And the carnival never stops.
Her long hands are two kites,
Trailing coloured tails of laughter,
Sketching, in the smoky air between us,
Whole galleries of portraits.
Frida Kahlo has been to dinner
And is now gone, taking the party with her,
Leaving this withered Puritan
Faded, dusty, unbearably alone.

S. Templeton

BEESWAX REMEMBERED

My nose greedy,
grasping for the fix
of buttery rich beeswax.
Yellow creamy orderliness
brings the comfort of
scratched key patterned
lino, mixed up with
the sharp smells from
the press in the lobby,
where I first breathed in
the dark rich blood
of the hare draining
into a bowl.
The thick brown soup
of my childhood,
taken for granted along
with firm white
whole King Edwards;
cutting, mashing them
through velvet strands.
I the guileless gourmet
supped it all up.

Gael Turnbull

PHOTOGRAPHS

Scarcely a year old, she looks out from a photograph and
laughs, instinctively and wholeheartedly, perhaps at the young
man who takes the photograph,

who may herself some day look at another photograph, taken
by her, of an old man who also laughs, if with fragmented
heart and after long consideration, enjoying the absurdity of
possibility and the resilience of paradox.

A WOMAN GOES TO VISIT

A woman goes to visit her bedridden mother. They talk about
the past while avoiding certain subjects. The mother suddenly
takes something from a bedside drawer. 'I want to be sure
you have it after I'm gone. I know how much it meant to you
when you were young.' It is a small brass frog. The woman
tries to control her panic as not only had she always thought
it inexpressibly ugly but that era of her childhood had been
far from happy.

Once again, she will have to dissemble and as ever the effort
will be flawed by saying too much and her mother will realise
she isn't being honest. But the mother misjudges, 'I know
you'd be affected. No need to say anything,' and closes her
eyes on the pillow, exhausted. The woman feels an immense
love and gratitude, such as she had rarely ever felt, that her
silence should have been so misunderstood.

IT'S BECAUSE

'It's because I love you so much,' he said, 'care about you,
can't stop thinking of you, wanting to look after you, make
sure you're safe, because

I can't bear not knowing where you are, who you're with,
what you're doing, all the time, everywhere, and only because
I love you, can't help loving you so much.'

Billy Watt

RESUSCITATION DUMMIES

Like the remnants
of a mad executioner
they come armless, legless
in swimming-cap hair.

Inspection reveals
the unblemished tautness
of their abdomens
plugged into meters

that will gauge the intimacy
of our kisses,
the brutality
of hand on sternum.

We are more intimate
with them
than with each other –
or with ourselves.

Around this hall
we bend over dummies,
trying to rehearse life
on the inanimate:

head tilt, jaw thrust,
cover nose or mouth
with a confidence
born of inconsequence...

Impelled by duty
or uncertainty,
we count the seconds
between each imagined pulse.

Brian Whittingham

A READING OF FORM

The Scottish poet

reads his Scottishy poems,
written in a form he understands
is essential.

'Not ... self gratifying *free verse*.'
He smirks a smidgen ... knowingly
when articulating the words ...
'free verse'

He reads each poem in Scots.
Then English.
Then Scots.

His minister-like voice
soothing

his congregation,
sitting on the book-shop floor,
leaning against shelves,
nursing book-launch ... red or white.
Still as stiff hardbacks.

His flock
nod their heads knowingly
as he stresses
the significance of syllable count,
with all the solemnity
his minister-like voice can muster.

Andrew Young

SHARING CIGARETTES

What I want to write about is that time you came on a flying visit from summer school, the weekend my parents were away. I remember I was supposed to meet you off the bus at seven. For once it was on time and I was late, and as I came up Margaret Street you were smoking beneath the Spectrum Centre, just where the shadows ended and the evening sunlight splashed the ground. Before I reached you you saw me and opened your arms for a hug, unhurried and unselfconscious, and we embraced until your cigarette smouldered into my coat. We were free. No-one was in town, there was nobody either of us had to phone or meet. I think we both felt the directionless possibilities of the evening ahead, because there was that slightly awkward, shy atmosphere we sometimes used to get between us, which we tried to compensate for by smiling into each other's eyes a bit too often. It only lasted one plate of rice in that new place by the river though, and by the time we had walked back up one of the vennels into town for our first drink, it had been blown away by the story-telling and piss-taking I loved in you from the start.

The pub on the corner of Church Street and Baron Taylor's Street was mobbed. In possession of the place were the ritual Friday drinkers, lads who had pretty obviously been on the sesh since leaving the surrounding offices at half past four. I seem to remember it taking ages to shove through to the bar, which was besieged by big twentysomethings in white shirts, the bloodflush in their impatient faces spreading slowly down through open collars. More of them were coming in by the minute, fed and freshened up, and greeted somewhat paradoxically as henpecked poofs by those who hadn't bothered going home. Did we get any notice taken of us that night? Probably; we frequently did.

– Hey Barry. Do that two look old enough to you to be in here, eh? Do they, eh?

– I don't think I know this pair. That young chappie there could do with a haircut and a nice shirt could he not, eh? Could you not, eh?

– What the fuck do you think you look like, eh? Do you think it's smart going around like that, eh?

You know the accent far too well for me to even attempt to transcribe *that*. Come to think of it, we never used to go into that place. Neither of us were particularly fond of juke-box led mass renditions of Tina Turner and Dr Hook. We must have chosen it because we didn't want to run into any chance faces from school, because we only wanted each other's company.

Typical, then, that after about half a pint, a guy came over and asked if he could join us. He seemed a bit too young to be your typical pub pain in the arse hanger-on, and in fact he wasn't, really. He certainly wasn't too drunk or anything, and just seemed a little out of things, a little sad. He didn't sound local and he said his name was Julian; that might have explained a lot. The guy was pretty generous at standing his round and everything, but I remember there were a couple of things I just didn't like about him. I remember, for example, that he seemed to address nearly all his comments exclusively to you, even though I was doing my usual, doing most of the talking and that. I also didn't like the way he just helped himself to your cigarettes without asking. I mean, I did that myself, but it's like, I didn't really smoke, and you could tell this guy definitely *did*. Anyway, after a round apiece, I wanted to go. Unusual for me to want to leave a pub before closing, but I had planned to see you on your own, and the guy with us didn't look like going anywhere. He seemed a bit put out when we said we were leaving, but it's not like we asked him to join us or anything, is it? You left him a couple of cigarettes to smoke, and we gave him the names of a couple of other decent pubs – the Haugh, the Market. I was pissed off about that – it knackered my chances of getting another drink anywhere. I didn't even think you should have bothered giving him the cigarettes, but you said it was alright, that we could get some more on the way up the road. And that's what we did, and we also got a couple of bottles of wine, and were home by ten. For once, none of the neighbours were walking their dogs, or putting the bins out, or adjusting that curtain which never seemed to hang right.

We placed the sticky wine glasses on the bedside table. I remember balancing on the mattress by the window, kissing softly, easily removing clothes in the shared knowledge that we had hours to do whatever we wanted to do; fucking slowly and damply on a bed made warm by the day's sun; later lying still entwined, sharing a Marlboro and sniggering breathlessly at the cliché, and the indulgence and the indulgence yet to come;

killing ourselves. I remember watching you sleep (as usual I couldn't): an arm draped on the quilt, the slightest pulse in your lips, a rogue piece of autumn-coloured fringe curling into one eye.

On the Saturday morning I got up while you were still sleeping and went out to buy things I thought would make a continental breakfast. I didn't bother switching on the local news, so I didn't know about the fuss in town until I came across it in Baron Taylor's Street. There was a crowd of shoppers around the paved courtyard behind the Bank of Scotland, which was sealed off with blue and white tape. Two police were standing just inside it; they were trying so hard to look aloof and responsible it was almost comic. But the most bizarre, cop-show element of the whole scene was something I just glimpsed between some shoulders as I pushed past: two sections of chalked or painted outline, a crude leg shape and part of an arm and hand, protruding from the shadows under the concrete steps.

When I got back and told you there had been a murder in town, you were far less curious than me.

– That's awful. What a shame. Never mind, though. What nice things have you got for us to eat?

So we forgot about it, and ate croissants, and ricotta, and smoked salmon, and crisp lettuce, and then water melon washed down with sparkling wine, all at eleven in the morning. I could still taste the sweetness of melon and wine, even with all the subsequent cigarettes, when I kissed you on to the Aberdeen bus a few hours later.

It wasn't until the report and the photo appeared in the Sunday papers that my curiosity was, I don't know if it was satisfied, or just exchanged for some other emotion.

Police have named the man stabbed to death in Inverness town centre on Friday night as Julian Deans, 25, of Elgin, Morayshire. Mr Deans, a chartered accountant, is thought to have been drinking alone in Inverness after completing some business in the town. Forensic experts have determined that the murder took place at approximately 10 p.m., and police are appealing for any possible witnesses, who may have been in the area at that time, to come forward. It is unclear whether the stabbing was a random attack, or whether there was provocation or perhaps a financial motive.

I'm not really sure why I never told you, except that I knew you never bothered with the news and the papers, and probably wouldn't find out from anyone else.

The local reaction or what I got of it, was predictably clichéd, hushed excitement masquerading as concern. You can probably hear the voices already, outside Eastgate, and Marks, and various kiltmakers.

– That's shocking, I don't know what it is with young people these days, the violence and the drugs and all that.

– Oh, right enough, right enough, but what I want to know is, what was the boy doing drinking on his own? There's something not quite right about that...

Despite the *Courier's* holier-than-thou editorial, there was no mistaking the slightly thrilled undertone that with this, its first downtown backstreets killing, the town had moved a bit closer to the city status which the council is always on about achieving. Little is known about the two fifteen year old boys who were charged with murder a couple of days afterwards; I think the trial is sometime later this year. Still less is known about Julian Deans.

But anyway, I didn't begin this to write about them. It occurred to me, looking back recently, that that was probably the last night we shared where things were as perfect as they had been at the start. Although the split took a while, after that things seemed to get a bit more strained and impatient. There were more excuses why we couldn't come and visit each other, and more tearful, trivial misunderstandings when we did, and what with us living in different towns, you doing new things, me doing the same as always... I suppose it was inevitable, and you know as much as I ever want you to know about how it went for me after that. But although it doesn't sound particularly remarkable written down – we didn't swim in the river at midnight, we didn't dance on the lawn under the moonlight, we didn't follow next door's Siamese cats to see where they would go – I do feel that that night was one of those perfect nights, one that should be immortalised as a memorial to what we had, and that's how I've tried to write it here. As it was, not as it has been in the dream I've had frequently since where you, sprawled asleep and gently living, fade to become a chalk outline on ash-grey slabs.

BIOGRAPHIES

Ingibjörg Ágústsdóttir was born in 1970 in the north-west of Iceland. She studied English Language and Literature at the University of Iceland and then moved to Scotland where she is currently working on a PhD thesis in Scottish Literature at Glasgow University. She writes poetry in both English and Icelandic.

Ken Angus was born in 1930 and is now semi-retired after a career in veterinary pathology. Some of his poems have been published in anthologies and magazines in Britain and Australia, and he recently won the top award in the Scots Language section of the Scottish International Open Poetry Competition.

Gavin Bowd was educated at Galashiels Academy and the University of St Andrews. He is the author of a booklet of poems, *Decades*, and an essay *The Outsiders: Alexander Trocchi and Kenneth White* (both Akros). His poetry, essays, fiction and translations have appeared in *Lines Review, Chapman, Edinburgh Review* and *Digraphe*.

Tom Bryan was born in Canada in 1950. Long-resident in Scotland, he lives in Wester Ross with his wife and two children and works part-time in pottery. Poet, fiction writer, he is widely published and broadcast. Poetry collections: *Wolfwind* (Chapman, 1996), *North East Passage* (Scottish Cultural Press, 1996). Former editor: *Northwards, Broken Fiddle*. Writing Fellow: Aberdeenshire 1994–1997. Widely anthologised.

Moira Burgess is a novelist, short story writer and literary historian. She has been working on the history of Glasgow fiction for some years, with two books, *Imagine a City* and *The Glasgow Novel: 3rd edition*, appearing in 1998, but is now getting back to writing fiction herself.

John Clifford is a playwright and translator. His plays include: *Losing Venice, Inés de Castro, Light in the Village, Great Expectations, Wuthering Heights*, and *Heaven Bent, Hell Bound*. His new libretto for *The Magic Flute* was premiered this year, along with his translation of *Life is a Dream*, which opened as part of the Edinburgh International Festival. He teaches drama at Queen Margaret College and lives in Edinburgh with his partner, Sue Innes, and their two daughters.

Ken Cockburn lives in Edinburgh. His first collection of poems, *Souvenirs and Homelands*, was published earlier this year by Scottish Cultural Press.

Stewart Conn lives in Edinburgh. Publications include *The Luncheon of the Boating Party* and *In the Blood* (Bloodaxe Books). His play *Clay Bull* was premiered in the Royal Lyceum Theatre earlier this year.

Robert Crawford's collections of poetry include *A Scottish Assembly* (Chatto, 1990), *Talkies* (Chatto, 1992), *Masculinity* (Cape, 1996), and *Sharawaggi* (with W.N. Herbert, Polygon, 1990). His new collection, *Spirit Machines*, will be published by Cape in 1999. He is Professor of Modern Scottish Literature at the University of St Andrews.

Allan Crosbie teaches in Edinburgh. He has had poems published in *Orbis* and *Cencrastus*.

Anna Crowe was born in 1945 in Plymouth. She is a St Andrews graduate (Modern Languages), living in St Andrews and working in a second-hand bookshop and as a creative-writing tutor. Prize-winner in National Poetry Competition, 1986. Winner of Peterloo Open Poetry Competition, 1993 and 1997. First collection, *Skating Out of the House* (Peterloo, 1997). Co-editor of *Fife Lines*.

Anne Donovan lives and teaches in Glasgow. Short stories published in *New Writing Scotland 14 & 15*, *A Braw Brew* and the *Flamingo Book of New Scottish Writing 1997 & 1998*. Winner of the *1997 Macallan/Scotland on Sunday* short story competition.

Gerrie Fellows was born in Roxburgh, New Zealand; one of the places which feature in *The Separations*, a sequence based on the placenames of the Scottish Diaspora. She now lives in Glasgow with her family. A previous collection, *Technologies*, was published by *Polygon*. She was Writing Fellow in Paisley 1993–95.

Jim Ferguson's collection *The Art of Catching a Bus and Other Poems* is published by Arc Press, Edinburgh. He is co-editor, with Bobby Christie, of Neruda Press.

Moira Forsyth lives in Dingwall. She has published poetry and short stories in magazines and anthologies and is review editor of *Northwards*. In 1996 she received a Writer's Bursary from the Scottish Arts Council.

Pete Fortune lives in Dumfries. His work has been widely published and broadcast on radio. SAC Writer's Bursary in 1995. With Liz Niven, currently putting together a book for Dumfries & Galloway Libraries to mark the Millennium. This is his sixth appearance in *New Writing Scotland*.

Raymond Friel's first collection of poems, *Seeing the River*, is published by Polygon. *Confiteor*, a poem-pamphlet, was published last year by Vennel Press. He is a co-editor of *Southfields*.

Iain Galbraith was born in Glasgow in 1956 and brought up at Arrochar. His poems, prose and essays have appeared in *Agenda, Ambit, Chapman, Gairfish, Liber, Lines Review, PN Review, Stand* and *2 Plus 2*. He is a freelance translator and has edited works by R.L. Stevenson and Joseph Conrad.

Valerie Gillies is a poet. Latest volume, *The Ringing Rock*. Commissions in 1998 include an artist's book with Will Maclean, *St Kilda Waulking Song* (Morning Star Press); sculpture panel text for the source of the Tweed; poetry for *Pax Romana* Exhibition, City Art Centre, Edinburgh Festival. Senior Hospital Arts Worker with Artlink.

Roddy Hamilton was born in 1965 in Musselburgh, Edinburgh, and lived in Barrhead and Inverurie before settling in Aberdeen where he now works as a Mac Designer for an advertising agency. He is shortly to embark on a tour of Britain, filming a video-diary, before completing his first novel.

George Gunn is a poet and playwright who was born in Thurso in 1956.

Brian Johnstone has lived and worked in Fife since 1969. A poet and photographer, his collection, *The Lizard Silence*, was published by Scottish Cultural Press in 1996. He was awarded a Scottish Arts Council Writer's Bursary in 1998. Founder of Edinburgh's *Shore Poets*, he is currently chairman of *Stanza '98*.

David Kinloch was born, brought up and educated in Glasgow. He is the author of *Paris-Forfar* (Polygon, 1994), was co-founder and co-editor of *Verse* and is co-editor of *Southfields*.

Norman Kreitman lives in Edinburgh and was formerly engaged in social and psychiatric research. His third poetry collection, *Butterfly Brown, Yellow*, will be published in Spring 1999 and he has recently completed a study of metaphor, also due for publication shortly.

Alex Laird spent his working life in the building industry, rising to a senior area management position, before moving to the Architects dept of a large local authority. Illness cut his working life short in his mid-fifties, and during the years when virtually confined to home, he began to write poetry. He is a member of his local writers' group.

Maurice Lindsay, now 80, a Glaswegian, trained as a musician, served during the 1939/40 war, latterly in the War Office Staff, was the first Programme Controller of Border Television, first Director of The Scottish Civic Trust, and from 1983 to 1990, Honorary Secretary-General of Europe Nostrum. Books include *Collected Poems 1940–90*, *The Burns Encyclopaedia* and, most recently, a collection of poems, *Speaking Likenesses*.

Gerry Loose is a poet and editor, who works both in agriculture and the arts. He was Writing Fellow for Glasgow City Council 1995–1997; he is currently Managing Editor for Survivors' Poetry Scotland. Publications include *Knockariddera; The Elementary Particles; a measure; A Holistic Handbook*.

Murdo M. MacDonald/Mac Mhurchaidh a Stal is presently working both as a dry-stone dyker, and as an archivist of the Sound Recordings and Photographic Collections of Canna Folklorists, John Lorne Campbell and his wife, Margaret Fay Shaw. He has recently returned to the Aberdeen area after having spent some time in Skye. Some of his poetry has been published in *Gairm* (since 1995); *New Writing Scotland 15* (1997); *Skinklin Star* (1998); *Poetry Scotland* (1998), and *Present Poets* (1998).

Carl MacDougall is a writer, reviewer and editor who has received awards, fellowships and bursaries.

Nicol Mackintosh was brought up in Fife and now lives and works in Edinburgh. He has contributed a number of short pieces to the Traverse Theatre's 'Monday Lizard' readings, but *Getting Started* is his first published story.

Ciara MacLaverty was born in Belfast in 1968 but has lived in Scotland since childhood. She attended Islay High School and went on to study Arts and Social Sciences at Glasgow University. Previous stories have appeared in *Cutting Teeth*, *West Coast Magazine* and *New Writing Scotland 15*.

Aonghas MacNeacail is a poet, scriptwriter, journalist and playwright who was born on the Isle of Skye in 1942.

John Maley was born in Glasgow in 1962. He has published poetry and a short story in previous editions of *New Writing Scotland*. Plays include *Witch Doctor* and *Daylight Robbery*. He is working on a short story collection set in and around a Glasgow gay bar.

John Manson was born in Caithness in 1932. Retired teacher. He has published poems and translations in Scots and English and critical essays in Scottish literature. Joint editor (with David Craig) of *Hugh MacDiarmid: Selected Poems* (Penguin, 1970, 1977). Complete translation of Victor Serge's *Carnets* (1944) into English on http://users.skynet.be/johneden (this year).

Brian McCabe is a poet and fiction writer. His publications include *One Atom To Another* (Polygon), *The Lipstick Circus* (Mainstream), *The Other McCoy* (Mainstream/Penguin), *In a Dark Room with a Stranger* (Hamish Hamilton/Penguin).

James McGonigal was born in 1947 and works in teacher education in Glasgow. He is currently co-editing two anthologies of verse: Scots-Irish and religious. *Driven Home* is the title poem of his second collection, forthcoming from Mariscat.

Hugh McMillan has had three books of poetry published, the latest, *Aphrodite's Anorak* (Peterloo) and his short stories have been anthologised here and abroad.

Gordon Meade was former Writing Fellow at Duncan of Jordanstone College of Art and Writer in Residence for Dundee District Libraries (1993/95). Most recent collection, *The Scrimshaw Sailor* (Chapman, 1996). Lives in the East Neuk of Fife with Wilma and their daughter, Sophie.

David Millar was born in Edinburgh in 1955. Previous short stories have been published by Rebel Inc., Clocktower Press and Edinburgh University Press. His play, *A Meeting with the Monster*, about Alexander Trocchi the controversial Scottish writer, was performed during the 1995 Edinburgh Fringe and at the Traverse Theatre in 1996.

William Neill, born 1922 in Ayrshire, writes in Gaelic, Scots and English. He has published several verse collections, one forthcoming with Luath Press. Work tends towards a satirical synthesis using the surviving tongues of Scotland.

Tom Pow's latest book was *Red Letter Day* (Bloodaxe, 1996). His next, *Transfusion*, is due from Bloodaxe next year.

Richard Price's first full-length collection of poems, *Perfume and Petrol Fumes*, will be published by Diehard in 1999. One of the 'Informationist' poets, his pamphlet *Marks & Sparks* was a *Scotland on Sunday* Critic's Choice. In 1997 he was short-listed for a Paul Hamlyn Foundation Award.

Suhayl Saadi is a British-Asian, Glasgow-based novelist and short story writer. In 1997, his first novel was published under a pseudonym and he won a major prize in the Bridport Short Story Competition. In between live readings and radio appearances (both on Community Radio and on BBC Radio Scotland), he is working on his fourth novel.

Adrian Salmond was born in Glasgow in 1972. He has had poems published in *Cutting Teeth, Affectionate Punch* and *Headlock*. Currently living in London, he works as a computer programmer.

Christine Stickland was born in Birmingham in 1941, married, had children, got divorced. After spending 22 years in Switzerland, she settled in North Berwick, joined the Writers' Group led by Dilys Rose, and began writing poetry again for the first time since her schooldays.

Sheila Templeton was born in Aberdeen, then spent an itinerant childhood ranging from North-East Scotland to Dar-es-Salaam. She left her grey granite roots thirty years ago to teach history near Edinburgh and has stayed there. Her poetry and prose often draw on the rich Buchan landscape of childhood.

Gael Turnbull's most recent publications include *A Rattle of Scree* (Akros) and *Transmutations* (Shoestring Press).

Billy Watt was born in Greenock and now lives in West Lothian, where he teaches at Broxburn Academy. His poetry booklet, *Porpoises on the Moray Firth*, was published last year and a short story selection, *Ways of Seeing, Ways of Falling*, is due out this year.

Brian Whittingham is a Glasgow poet. Previous collections: *Premier Results* (with Magi Gibson); *Swiss Watches*; *The Ballroom Dancer*; *Ergonomic Workstations*; *Spinning Teacans* and *Industrial Deafness*.

Andrew Young was born in 1973 and grew up in Inverness. He is currently completing a PhD in 'The Scottish Small Town Novel' at Glasgow University. *Sharing Cigarettes* is his first published short story.